EARLY FORGED STAMPS DETECTOR

by

Thornton Lewis
Edward Pemberton
Thomas Dalton

SANFORD J. DURST
Numismatic & Philatelic Publications
New York, N.Y.

133 East 58th Street
New York, N.Y. 10022

LC NO. 79-50611

ISBN 0-915262-39-8

Originally published as
Forged Stamps & How to Detect Them
by Thornton Lewis and Edward Pemberton
Edinburgh — 1863
and
How to Detect Forged Stamps
by Thomas Dalton
Gateshead — 1865

FORGED STAMPS:

HOW TO DETECT THEM,

BY

THORNTON LEWES AND EDWARD PEMBERTON.

CONTAINING ACCURATE DESCRIPTIONS OF ALL
FORGED STAMPS.

EDINBURGH:
PRINTED BY COLSTON & SON, 80 ROSE STREET.

MDCCCLXIII.

CONTENTS.

—o—

P-315

FOREWORD TO THE REPRINT

One great problem plaguing the philatelist has always been the proliferation of counterfeits of better grade stamps. Today of course for historical and monetary reasons, these include many of the issues of the first two decades of stamp production, being rare, and valuable issues.

Most interesting however is the fact that forgeries were a problem from the very beginning, as evidenced by the two books reprinted here, published originally in 1863 and 1865 respectively. Notice the large number of counterfeits produced even then, many of which may still survive (in relation to the number of genuine specimens) of early postal emissions.

It is with great pleasure, and a feeling of contribution to the philatelic collector/investor and dealer that we republish this valuable guide with the hope that its availability will produce the desired results of ridding the world of those existing early forgeries that still exist.

SANFORD J. DURST
Publisher

INTRODUCTION.

———o———

It has long been evident to collectors of postage stamps, that a really accurate description of all forgeries is as great a necessity as even a catalogue of genuine stamps. As Mr Mount Brown has amply provided for the latter want, we cannot but think that the results of our investigations (contained in this volume) must be of the greatest use to those engaged in the interesting pursuit of stamp collecting. We have tested the uselessness of the only English work on the "Falsification of Postage Stamps," having gone through it carefully, and after an impartial reading, feel convinced that, from the vagueness of the descriptions, both of the forgeries and genuine stamps, many persons testing stamps from them, would select the forgery as genuine, and *vice versâ*. The best proof of this is, that many of the forgeries described in the work have been sent to us as genuine by the translator and the author, than which no better proof could be had of the uselessness of the work; for if those who wrote and translated it were unable to detect the forgeries from their own descriptions, others can hardly be expected to do so.

Collectors are naturally curious as to the origin of forgeries. Who forges them? and when were they first forged? are questions which suggest themselves to the enquiring mind. We will do our best to give a little information on these points. First and foremost among stamp forgers, is one at Zurich (well known to us), from whom emanate those which have had the largest circulation, viz. the Swiss, and probably the provisional Modena, the Romagna, and the Tassa Gazzette (Modena). Collectors have the greatest difficulty in obtaining anything like fair prices or exchanges for genuine specimens of any of the above, owing to the low prices at which the forgeries are obtainable, and the large circulation they have had. The prices charged by the agent (in Basle) of this Zurich dealer are, for most of the Swiss, 80 cts. each used, or unused 1 franc; for the Orts Post and Poste Locale, 50 cts. each; for Modena and Romagna 80 cts. The dealer who occupies the second position in our estimation is the proprietor of the provisional Parma, Modena (9 c. B. G. and 1 lira principally), provisional Naples, Spain (1 cuarto), and perhaps the Romagna. He is a dealer in Brussels. His forgeries have been sold largely, and are well executed. These two are the principal forgers, those indeed who have made almost a trade of it. There is a dealer in Brunswick who tried his hand at the Danish Essays; the results were good as regards execution, but the colour was too blue, and the brown became nearly orange. Whether the really beautiful imitations of the Danish Essays which have been so largely sold and exchanged (doubtless unknowingly) by Mr Erik Ritzau of Copenhagen, may be attributed to the Brunswick dealer, is not likely to be known. Doubtless other dealers besides the above three have forged stamps, but their efforts seem to have been confined principally to those which are easily changed in colour by acids, seldom venturing on the more difficult art of forgery. A few stamps are, we believe, forged in Leipsic. If so, the Argentine originate there, but the forger is unknown to us.

In answering the next query, how long have stamps been forged? we have to enquire into the time that collecting has gone on. We find that six or seven years ago, collectors were very few and far between, and on enquiring further back, the pursuit seems to have been confined to three or four gentlemen (certainly very few more); but about five years since, when the number of stamps had increased so much as to attract some little attention, the number of collectors began to increase; still they could only be counted by units, and it was not till three years after, that stamp collecting became anything like the general practice it now is. Probably forging was little thought of till about two years since, when the "mania" for the coloured pieces of paper began to extend so much that the rarer sorts were commanding a certain price. Still, very little could have been done in them. One of the first forgeries seems to have been Neuchâtel, 5c., which was sent to us from Baden about eighteen months since; further back than that, it is difficult to trace them. Last May the trade in false stamps must have received a decided impetus—or what is as probable, the forgers had grown bolder—for false stamps of all kinds began to come over from the continent in some quantities; and from that time to the present, they have gone on increasing in number, to an extent that has made it quite unsafe to accept any rare obsolete stamp (especially if unused), without comparison with undoubtedly genuine specimens. The same is the case with stamps pretending to be just issued, which should not be taken without the opinion of some friend qualified to give one. Of course care should be taken with these latter, not to reject them *too* hastily, for stamps might be refused which there would be great difficulty in obtaining afterwards. It is not always possible to obtain the loan of undoubtedly genuine stamps for the purpose of comparison, and there being no work (of any use) on the subject of forgeries, we have tried to supply these two wants in the present volume by making our descriptions of the real and false stamps so clear, that a collector having a single specimen of any stamp may determine as to its genuineness, without any other aid than our descriptions. This has often been very difficult, for we have to describe an almost imperceptible difference in such a manner that it cannot be misunderstood; for we know, that unless the descriptions are very clear indeed, mistakes will arise, and then the book would be at once condemned as nearly useless.

From the perusal of the following pages it will be seen that we have had no easy task, having had to get to the bottom of many misconceptions, and being often led astray by false information from those whose interest it was to suppress the truth. That this work (small as it is) is free from errors, we can hardly flatter ourselves, but we have spared no trouble or expense in obtaining reliable information. The forgeries from which the descriptions are taken, have cost us a great deal, as we have often had to buy them at the rate of genuine stamps, or we should have been unable to obtain them.

The most natural way of classifying false stamps, is :—

I. Forgeries in imitation of genuine stamps.

II. Stamps entirely fictitious, those which never had an existence except in the imagination of the originator.

III. Stamps not even intended as forgeries, but which, from some misconception, have been acknowledged as legitimate stamps by some collectors.

Division I. is the largest, but requires no explanation. Division II. contains, first, stamps made from the imagination, as Turkish 6 truzi, &c.; and, secondly, stamps which have been changed in colour by chemical agency, comparatively common ones serving for this purpose. Division III. is also very clear, containing the so-called Iceland, Danish 3 thiele, &c. As this work must fall into the hands of some of the forgers, we expect it will have the effect of making them issue fresh forgeries of the stamps mentioned here, and in which the slight differences whereby they may now be known from the originals will be entirely removed, so we must caution our readers to exercise the greatest care in buying or exchanging scarce stamps, and not to accept stamps as genuine and just issued which are not found in Mount Brown's third edition of his catalogue, or in the notices of new stamps in the "Stamp Collector's Review," or in the "Stamp Collector's Magazine," in both of which the earliest notices appear. We have devoted a small portion of our space to a review of stamps of which no definite information can be collected. The reader may wonder why this has been introduced in a work on "Forged Stamps," but a perusal of our reasons at the commencement of this notice will perfectly explain it. Collectors having stamps of which they have any suspicions (we allude to those not herein described) are earnestly requested to forward such specimens to either of our addresses mentioned below. They will be at once returned to the owners with full information as to their genuineness or otherwise, and all those stamps will be published in a second edition, should the demand for the present one justify another. For convenience of reference, an index has been added, and as some guide to collectors, we give the prices that *genuine* copies of any of the forgeries described may reasonably fetch.

With this short introduction we will set out on our undertaking, just hinting that a good magnifying glass has proved of great assistance to us in our researches, and recommending the use of one to all our readers who wish to test stamps from our descriptions.

EDWARD L. PEMBERTON,
Beaufort Road,
Edgbaston,
BIRMINGHAM.

THORNTON A. LEWES,
4 Duncan Street,
Drummond Place,
EDINBURGH.

PART I.

STAMPS FORGED FROM DIES IN IMITATION OF GENUINE STAMPS.

ARGENTINE CONFEDERATION.

1861. Name, Arms (rising sun with Cap of Liberty).
5 centavos red, 10 c. green, 15 c. blue.

Genuine.	*Forged.*
The hands are clasped together, and hold a *small staff*, on the top of which is a *cap of liberty*.	The hands are much more distinct than in the genuine one, but the *staff and cap of liberty are wanting*.
The glory round the head is *not thick*, but *straggling*.	The glory round the head is *very thick*.
The colours are *bright*, but *not remarkably so*.	The colours are *intensely* bright.

BAVARIA.

Figure, indicating value, in a circle.
3 kr. black.

The figure 3 is solid throughout, without veining in it. The word "Drei" is at the right hand, "Franco" at the bottom, and "Kreuzer," at the left hand. This is a wretchedly executed lithograph, and an impudent forgery. No such stamp ever existed. There is also a photograph of the old 1 kreuzer in circulation.

CAPRERA.

The following barefaced forgery is now being sold in London as a Caprera stamp. It is hardly necessary to say that there never have been stamps for that island. We borrow the description from Dr Gray:—"It was a water-colour drawing, somewhat like the Tuscan arms and crown; but the frame was inscribed, 'Postale Caprera Italia' (which means nothing, the literal translation is 'Postal Caprera Italy'), 1 scudo, and dated 1.8.6.0 in the angles. The letters are painted on with white lead, instead of being left white by the printing, as they would be in a real stamp."

CONFEDERATE STATES OF AMERICA.

1861. Name, Head of Jefferson Davis to right in oval.
5 cents green, 5 cents blue, 5 cents red, 5 cents black.

It is doubtful whether the 5 cents red and black were ever issued; they may be inventions of the forgers; at least, no stamped specimens have ever come under our notice. It should be remarked that these stamps were not intended originally to cheat collectors. They are sold in the shops in New York as imitations of the Southern stamps, and the words "Counterfeit Confederate Stamps," or something to that effect, are printed at the bottom of the sheet. But American collectors and dealers have sent them over in great quantities as genuine.

Genuine.	*Forged.*
The hair on head does not go up to the words, there being a space, in some places broader, in others narrower, all round.	The hair on head goes up to the words "Confederate States of America;" from the D to the S of "Confederate States," it almost touches the letters.
The words "Postage" and "Five Cents" are in stout compact printing.	The words are in thin letters, rather wide apart.
Bold and well done, but rather indistinct.	Looks rough and unfinished, but very clear.
The background is composed of very *fine close lines*, and looks almost solid.	The background is *coarse*, the lines being *wide apart*, and *distinct*.
The "C" of "Confederate," and the last "a" of "America," are on a *level* with the mouth.	The "C" of "Confederate," and the last "a" of "America" on a *level* with the *nose*.
The face is *dotted all over*.	The face is only dotted on the *right of the forehead* and *right cheek*, and a *little* on the *left cheek*.
The portrait of Davis is like, the face is long, and the expression is that of intense energy.	The face is round, and looks stupid, without any particular expression.

10 cents, pink and blue.

No genuine specimen has fallen into our hands, so that unfortunately we cannot give a description of it. As almost all the other local Confederate stamps sold by dealers are forged, and we have no genuine specimens to compare them with, we are obliged merely to give their names, without any description. This we hope to remedy in a future edition.

They are:

Memphis, " Paid 5 cents" (pink).
Mobile Post Office, 5 cents Paid (blue).
Baton Rouge, 5 cents, P. O. J. M'Cormick, (red and green)
M. C. Callaway, Paid 2 cents (blue).

DENMARK.

Essays, with head of Mercury, value 4 R.B.S., $1\frac{1}{4}$ sch. c.; with head of King, value 8 R.B.S., $2\frac{1}{2}$ sch. c.
Brown, on a ground composed of diagonal blue strokes.

Genuine.	*Forged.*
The wavy border, which contains the inscription, *touches the outer line in* 8 *places.*	The wavy border *does not touch the outer line at any point*, there being always a narrow space betweent hem.
The circle of dots surrounding head, *projects* into the wavy border under the letters K. G. L.	The circle of dots *does not project* into the border.
The right hand wing of Mercury's head, *i.e.* the one farthest off, is higher than the nearer one in its whole length, so that a *narrow border of the former is seen everywhere.*	Only the *top* and *end* of the far-off wing *are visible*, the near wing projecting into the other.
The figure 4 is like the *written* figure.	The figure 4 is like the *printed* figure.
The letter H in Sch is on *a level* with the others.	The letter H is *higher* than the others.
The King's ear is only *half visible*, the top being covered by the hair.	The King's ear is *completely uncovered.*
The beard is *very short*, and *hardly projects* below the chin.	The beard is *long* and pointed, and *projects considerably* below the chin.
The nose is *round* at the point, and there is *no shading* on the chin at the side of the beard.	The nose is *pointed*, and the chin is *strongly shaded.*
The hair is curly *all over.*	The hair is only curled *at the end.*
The King's neck is *turned up at front and back.*	The King's neck is *not turned up.*

We have not separated these two stamps, as, except in the heads, they are exactly alike, so that one description suffices for both.

These stamps have the diagonal blue lines usually very faint, but sometimes bright, nevertheless, if they are very bright, the stamps are probably forged.

GRANADA CONFEDERATION.

1861—Name, arms in shield, with words "Estados unidos de Nueva Granada" in oval, and in bordering the words "Correos nacionales." 2½ centavos, black.

Genuine.	*Forged.*
Nine stars under inscription.	*No* stars under inscription.
The letters of the inscription are *long and thin*, and all of the *same height*.	The letters of the inscription are *thick* and *unequal*.
The shield is divided into three compartments; the top and bottom ones are *shaded with black lines*, the *middle* one is *white*.	The shield is divided into *three white* compartments.
In the upper division is a helmet and flags.	In the upper division is a cornucopiæ.

MODENA.

Name (Estensi), eagle under crown, surrounded by wreath. 5 c. green, 9 c. B. G. light purple, 10 c. pink, 15 yellow, 25 brownish yellow, 40 c. blue, 1 lira white.

These stamps are forged from two different dies, probably made at different places, so that if one description does not suit the specimen under examination, the collector must try the other.

We would particularly advise collectors to examine the 9 c. B. G. and the 1 lira when offered them cheap, as both, when genuine, will fetch high prices.

Genuine.	*Forged.*
Tail of eagle is *very thin* at the point where the legs separate, and it *does not touch* the legs.	The tail of the eagle is of the *same thickness* throughout, and *touches* the legs.
The crown *does not touch* the eagle's head.	The crown *touches* the eagle's head.
The neck is *narrow* under the beak, and gradually grows thicker towards the body.	The neck is *very thick* (unnaturally so) across, under the beak.
The whole appearance of the eagle is neat, and the feathers are well defined.	The eagle is all blotched, and very dark under the white tips of the wings and at the tail.

Second kind.

Genuine.	*Forged.*
These stamps are printed on *unglazed* paper.	These stamps are printed on *glazed* paper.
Both of the upper joints of the eagle's legs stand out equally from the body.	The left hand upper joint of the eagle's leg is almost in a line with the outline of the body, while the right one projects considerably.
The white space at the top of the wings is *kidney shaped.*	*No white space* at the top of the *left wing*, and a long *sinuous* one on the *right wing.*
	The body of the eagle on the left side is very fat, and out of proportion.
The letters in the inscription are long and thin, and nearly reach to the black lines above and below.	The letters in the inscription are thick and smudged, and considerably shorter.
The branches surrounding the eagle *do not touch* the black line above the value.	The branches surrounding the eagle *touch* the black line above the value.
The eagle's claws are *long*, thin, and *distinct.*	The claws are *short* and *indistinct.*
The black stroke, representing the bottom joint of the leg, is *straight.*	The black stroke, representing the bottom joint of the leg, is *bent.*
The leaves are *thin and neat.*	The leaves are *thick.*
The ornaments in the border *do not touch* the enclosing lines.	The ornaments in the border *touch* the enclosing lines in two or three places.

MODENA.

Tassa Gazzette (Newspaper stamp), black on white.
Small square containing eagle, value, 10 centesimi.

This stamp it is almost impossible to describe, the only difference being in the body of the eagle, where, in the genuine stamp, the feathers are represented by short thick lines, whereas, in the forgery, they are represented by long thin lines. But let the collector bear in mind that the genuine stamp is *coarsely* executed on greyish unglazed paper, whilst the forgery is *neatly* done on blueish glazed paper, and he will be at once able to tell whether a specimen is genuine or not.

MODENA.

Provisional Government.

1859. Name (Modonesi), Savoy cross in shield under crown.
5 c. green, 15 chocolate, 20 blue, 40 pink, 80 yellow.

Genuine.	*Forged.*
The ornament at corners is composed of two straight lines cutting each other diagonally at right angles, with three points at each end. (This is not always clear.)	The ornament at corners consists of four three-pointed strokes, with a small circle in the middle.
The shield is divided into four *equal* fields by the *cross*, which is *not quite perpendicular.*	The shield is divided into four *unequal* fields, of which the bottom right hand one is the smallest. The *cross* is *quite perpendicular.*
The colours are *faint*, and the stamps printed on thin *white unglazed* paper.	The colours are *bright*, and the paper is *blueish* and *glazed.*

N.B. It should be remarked that the genuine 15 is chocolate, and the forgery black.

NAPLES.

Provisional Government.

October 1860. ½ tornese blue. Arms, (three legs and three fleurs-de-lis).

This stamp is the ½ grano of the old issue, with the "G" turned into a "T." But this has not succeeded well, as there is always a blotch about the "T," which, if closely examined, will be found to be part of the "G."

Genuine.	*Forged.*
In the bottom white line, nearly under the ½, is *a small "G,"* probably the initial of the engraver. (This is found in all the oldest set.)	The letter "*G*" *is wanting.*
At the juncture of the three legs there is *a head.*	The *head is wanting* at the juncture of the legs.
Letter "T" (as mentioned above), is *blotched.*	The letter "T" is *quite clear.*

Nov. 1860. ½ tornese, blue. Arms, (Savoy cross.)

Genuine.	*Forged.*
In the bottom white line under the ½, is the engraver's initial, "G," very small.	The "G" is wanting.
The outline of the three legs, fleurs-de-lis, and other parts of the other ½ tornese, are *seen more or less distinctly* through the cross.	The stamp being from a different die, *has no traces* of the legs, &c.
The letter "T" is *blotched.*	The letter "T" is *not blotched.*

NASHVILLE.

1861. Name, stars, and figure indicating value in oval, encircled by W. D. M'Nish, P.M., Tenn.

5 cents crimson, 5 cents grey on blue.

The 5 cents grey is possibly altogether fictitious.

Genuine.	*Forged.*
The word "Paid" is in *long* letters close together.	The word "Paid" is in *short* letters, farther apart.
The star to the right of word "Paid" is *on a level* with the word.	The star to the right of word "Paid" is *rather above* the word.
All the letters in "Tenn." the same size.	The letters "nn" are smaller than "Te."
Top star is *just over* "*ai*" in "Paid."	Top star *more over the* "*a*" *than the* "*i*" in "Paid."
The stamp is printed *indistinctly* and *smudged;* the ornaments in the corners are well done.	*Clean* and very *distinct*, especially the ornamentation in the corners, but the latter is badly done
The border consists of *one white narrow line.*	The border consists of *one very thin* and *another very broad* white line.
	The forgery is much larger than the original.
The stars are *thick.*	The stars are *thin.*

New Orleans.

1861. Name, figure indicating value in centre, encircled by "New Orleans Post Office," and bearing the name of J. L. Riddell at top and bottom.

2 cents blue, 5 cents brown, 2 cents red.

The 2 cents red is possibly fictitious.

5 cents brown.

Genuine.	*Forged.*
The hyphen joining "New-Orleans" *touches the* "*O.*"	The hyphen *does not touch* the "O."
The ornament at the left hand bottom corner has only *three* points.	The ornament at the left hand bottom corner looks like an arm with *four* fingers.
The white ornament under the letter "P" of "Paid" looks like a horse's neck and head.	The ornament is a badly formed crescent.
The word "Post" and the "ce" of "Office" touch the line above them.	None of the letters touch the line above.
The right hand top ornament has 5 dots inside	The right hand top ornament has no dots.

2 cents blue.

Genuine.	*Forged.*
All the printing is thick and coarse, and the whole stamp is indistinct. The colour is a pale greenish blue.	The printing is thin and neat, and the stamp extremely clear. The colour is a bright blue.

NICARAGUA.

1862. Mountains, with cap of liberty.
5 centavos black.

A person in London is now selling at 1s. each representations of this stamp. Although he tells everybody that they are merely fac-similes, and not the real stamps, we cannot but help thinking that he is acting wrongly; for less scrupulous dealers than himself will sell them as genuine; thus collectors will have to examine each Nicaragua stamp they may get, very carefully. Again, these imitations are by far the best executed of any we have seen. The regularly forged stamps are wretched in comparison with these, and, therefore, all the more caution will be required to detect them. We give the difference :—

Genuine.	*Imitation.*
Figure 5 in the corners, short and very broad.	Figure 5 in the corners, longer and narrow.
The letters "C" in "Cinco" are exactly like the "C" in "Centavos."	The top of the "C" in "Cinco" is singularly elongated.
Front mountain lower than the second, black one.	The front mountain is almost on a level with the other.
The tip of the cap hangs over without touching the rest of the cap.	The tip touches the cap.
The letters are all very thick, and the "N" and "i" of "Nicaragua" touch each other.	The letters are thinner, do not touch each other.

PARMA.

Provisional Government.

1861. 5 c. green, 6 c. red, 9 c. blue, 10 c. brown, 20 blue, 40 red, 80 yellow.

Genuine.	*Forged.*
The middle line in the border is *closer to the outside* than to the inside line.	The middle line is either *just in the middle*, between the two other lines, or nearer to the inside line.
The letters "c" and "i" in word "Centesimi," *do not touch* the border.	The letters "c" and "i" in word "Centesimi" *almost touch* the border.

All the 8 *lines* forming the border are *more or less concave.*	The 4 *short lines* (one at each corner) forming the border, are *quite straight*, the four longer ones concave.

ROMAGNA.

1861. ½ yellow, 1 grey, 2 yellow, 3 green, 4 red, 5 purple, 8 pink, 20 blue.

Genuine.	*Forged.*
All the letters are *sharp* at the corners, and the letters of the word "Romagne" have small, *sharply defined indentations.*	The letters are more or less *round* at the corners, and the *indentations* in word "Romagne" *irregular and not sharply defined.*
Ornaments in the corners, composed of *thin* lines.	Ornaments in corners *thick* and blotched.
At each corner of the ornaments is a black dot, though occasionally one of them is wanting at a corner.	At the left hand bottom corner ornament, there are no black dots.
The two stops after word "Bai," *square.*	The two stops after word "Bai," *round.*
These stamps are printed on *rather rough unglazed* paper.	Printed on *smooth slightly glazed* paper.

SANDWICH ISLANDS.

1860. Name (Hawaiian Postage), figure indicating value.
1 cent blue.

Genuine.	*Forged.*
The letter "C" in "Cents" is *very broad*, and all the letters are thin and neat.	The letter "C" in "Cents" is *not remarkably broad*, and the letters are thicker and smudged.
The figure 1 is firm and neat, the stroke at the top of it is thick and long.	The figure 1 not so clearly defined; the stroke at the top is thin and short.

This stamp is so simple in design, that it is extremely difficult to describe differences, which will be best understood by comparison with nndoubtedly genuine specimens. It should, however, be borne in mind that if the letters are very clear, and the letter "C" remarkably broad, the stamp is probably genuine.

2 cents black.

Genuine.	*Forged.*
The figure 2 is elegantly executed. The little black line at the left hand bottom corner points to the letter "C" in "Cents."	The figure 2 is wretchedly done. The top hangs over in an ungraceful curve, the body ought to be thicker, and the little black line at

	the left hand bottom corner of the figure, points to the figure 2 at the bottom.
The letter "C" in "Cents" *remarkably broad.*	The letter "C" in "Cents" *not remarkably broad.*
After the word "Cents" there is a *large* full stop.	After the word "Cents" there is a *small* full stop.

1860. Blue 5 cents. Bust of King Kamehameha III.

Genuine.	*Forged.*
The letter "S" in "Cents" is *perpendicular.*	The letter "S" in "Cents" *falls over* to the left.
The king's nose, formed on the left side, by a *curved line.*	*No line* on the nose, which is merely indicated by dots.
The whole face but the nose is dotted, so as to leave no white space.	There is a white space, free from dots under left side of mouth.
The leaves on the king's coat are long, and at a proper distance from each other.	The leaves on the king's coat are shorter and very close to each other.
At the side of the leaves is a row of *six buttons, white, and very distinct.*	The buttons are very *indistinct,* only three or four *can be counted* with certainty.
Background composed of crossed lines, very dark and close to each other.	The lines are wider apart.
The collar is loose and open in front. There is a dark blue triangular space between the two ends of the collar and the chin.	The collar is tighter, and closed, or nearly so, in front.
On the king's right arm, *i.e.*, in the left hand corner, is a white spot, all the rest of the arm being shaded off.	On each arm there is a distinct white line, contrasting strongly with the background where it touches it.
On the blue line above the words "Five Cts." *are two little blue dots,* one just over the end of the "F," and other between the "T" and "S."	*No blue dots.*

The forgery is usually printed on white paper, whereas the genuine one is commonly on blue paper. The genuine impression on white paper is very rare.

There is also a photograph of the 5 cents, brownish black, in circulation.

SPAIN.

1850. Correo Interior. 1 cuarto bronze. Bear on Tree.

Genuine.	*Forged.*
The horizontal strokes between the octagonal shield and the square containing, are *nine on each side.*	On the right hand side, both top and bottom, there are *ten* strokes (counting the point in the corner),

	on the left hand top at the there are *eleven*, and in the bottom one *nine*.
The top bunch of leaves on the right side in the wreath contains *three long* leaves.	The top bunch on the right side contains *three short and thin* leaves.
The second bunch contains *four* leaves, and the third likewise.	The second bunch contains *three* leaves, and the third likewise.
On the left side the bottom bunch contains *three* long leaves.	The bottom one on the left side contains *four* short leaves.
On the top of the crown is a *little cross*.	There is *no cross* on the crown.
The figure 1 is of the same height as the words.	The figure 1 is longer than the words.
The foliage is dark on the right side and light on the left.	The foliage is equally shaded throughout.
Only *one* of the *bear's arms* is visible.	*Both* of the *bear's arms* are visible.

SWITZERLAND.

1850. I. Orts Post. 2½ rappen, for the German Cantons.

Genuine.	*Forged.*
The stamp is printed on *dull white* paper.	The stamp is printed on *faintly bluish tinged* paper.
The black wavy line in right hand top corner touches the label containing the superscription, *over the letter "T."*	The black wavy line in right hand top corner, touches the label containing the superscription, *between "S" and "T."*
The thick line enclosing the white scroll is alternately white and black.	The line enclosing the white scroll is much thinner, and the colours do not alternate equally, the right hand side being often quite black.
It does not touch the border of the stamp.	On the left side it touches the border of the stamp.

1850. II. Poste Locale. 2½ rappen, for the French Cantons.

Genuine.	*Forged.*
The stamp is printed on *white* paper.	The stamp is printed on faintly *blueish tinged* paper.
Under "2½" and "Rp." is a *small curved perpendicular line.*	The *line is wanting*,
The line enclosing the white scroll does *not touch* the border of the stamp.	The line enclosing the white scroll *touches* the left hand border of the stamp.

Wavy black line in left hand top corner *does not touch* the border of the stamp.	Wavy black line in left hand top corner *touches* the border of the stamp.

III. BASLE.

1850. Dove, in white relief, on red shield.

Genuine.	*Forged.*
Ground composed of alternate *blue and white dots.*	Ground of a *uniform pale green.*
The figures "$2\frac{1}{2}$," and word "Rp." are very thin.	The figures "$2\frac{1}{2}$," and word "Rp." are almost as thick as the inscription.
The key is of the same thickness above and below the middle rings.	The key is very much thicker below the middle rings than above.
The middle bottom point of the key is *long*, and almost touches the black line.	The middle bottom point of the key is *short*, and a good distance from the black line.
Both the outside bottom points of the key *touch* the side black lines.	The *outside left hand* bottom point *touches*, and the *right hand* one does *not touch*, the side black line.

IV. GENEVA.

These stamps are forged in greater numbers than perhaps any others, and it is almost impossible to give descriptions, because the genuine ones often differ considerably from each other. As will be seen from the following pages, the light green is forged from two different dies, one being an imitation of the light green 5, and one an imitation of the dark green 5.

There are five Geneva Stamps—5 c. dark green; 5 c. light green (considerably smaller than the other, and without a crown); 5 c. green on white; 5 c. black on white (Essay); all these are Port Cantonal; and the small 5 c. Port Local.

We do not know whether the black one has ever been forged; should a forgery of it turn up, it shall be at once described. Suffice it, that it resembles the 5 c. Port Cantonal light green, in *not having the crown.*

The 5 c. green on white, as before remarked, it is impossible to describe; the forged ones, however, are usually on bluish white paper, whereas the genuine ones are on white paper.

The 5 c. dark green, it is likewise impossible to describe, so exact is it that we are almost sure that the original die has come into the possession of one of the forgers, and that the stamps are printed off it. The only difference consequently is in the paper. This, in all the genuine ones, is an intensely dark blue-green. The forgers have printed various stamps from this die on yellowish and pale-green paper, but these are all fictitious.

The 5 cents light green, again, is also very variable, no two specimens being exactly alike. There is, therefore, nothing else to be done with these Geneva, but to compare them with others, or get the advice of some person who knows them. We shall be most happy to give our opinion upon any that may be sent for inspection.

5 c. Port Local.

Genuine.	*Forged.*
The rays are very equal and do not go beyond " de " in inscription. The top feather of eagle's wing is curved upwards, and the foot touches it.	The rays are unequal, extending to the right hand more than to the left. The top feather of the eagle's wing is curved to the left, and the foot of eagle does not touch it.

This stamp is extremely scarce genuine ; almost every specimen in this country being forged.

The 10 c. Geneva Port Cantonal, composed of two 5 c. Port Local, is a complete fiction. One would think its appearance was enough to condemn it, and yet it has been largely sold, and even inserted in our best catalogue of stamps. As before remarked, it consists of two Port Local stamps (wider than the usual forgery) printed in black on dingy-green paper, and connected at the top by a label, in which is printed " 10 Port Cantonal Cent." The Stamps are Port Local (both of them) and yet the label at the top has Port Cantonal on it ! To this it may be objected, that the 5 c. Port Local were all printed together thus, so that two could be used for the Canton, or if only one was required for a town letter, it could be cut out and used separately. We ourselves have heard this stated. But if it be borne in mind, that a *Cantonal* letter never cost more than 5 centimes, unless overweight, as the 5 centimes Cantonal stamps abundantly show, there could have been no reason for a stamp for double that amount.

V. NEUCHATEL.

Poste Locale, 5 centimes.
1850. White Cross on red ground, black impression.

Genuine.	*Forged.*
The three-pointed ornament at each side of the label containing the value, is *narrower* than the label.	The three-pointed ornament at each side of the label containing the value, is *as broad as* the label.
The label containing the superscription is a good distance from the top of the stamp.	The label containing the superscription is close to the top.
Exactly in the middle, above the label, are two little circles, which fill out the space between the label and the top of tho stamp, and on each side of these circles is a well defined curve.	The space between, is filled out by three or four little strokes.

VI. VAUD.

Poste Locale, 4 c., 5 c. black on white.
1850. Small rectangle, White Cross on red ground, with Post Horn.

Genuine.	*Forged.*
The left end of the post horn is *elongated*, and almost touches the black border of the scroll.	The left end of the horn is *not elongated*, and is further off from the border of the scroll.
The words "Poste Locale" long and firm.	The words "Poste Locale" are short and smudged.
The folds encircling the post horn and binding it to the ring containing the cross come, on the left hand side, up to the middle of the large black dot, *i.e.*, the top one of the four dots, which are placed in a curve round the label containing the value.	The folds encircling the post horn and binding it to the ring containing the cross, do not come up to the black dot.
The top ornament, on both sides of the superscription, overhangs the lower ornament considerably.	The top ornament, on both sides of the superscription, does not overhang, or scarcely so, the second ornament.
The highest large black dot under the horn, on the right side, is as big as the two under ones.	The highest large black dot under the horn, on the right side, is smaller than the two under ones.
The horn on the right side is *thin*, and the top is slightly turned *outwards*.	The horn, on the right side, is *thicker*, and the top is turned *inwards*.

There is another forgery, executed from a different die, but very badly done; there are only three dots on the right side under the horn; the horn is very thick and very strongly turned inwards, the cross is very small, and the whole stamp is coarsely printed.

VII. ZURICH.

1843. 4 rappen, 6 rappen.

Superscription (Zurich) value indicated by large figure in the centre. At the bottom of the 4 rappen are the words "Local Taxe;" at that of the 6 rappen, "Cantonal Taxe." Date indicated by one figure in each corner, thus :—1. 8. 4. 3.

1843. Like the above, but with date only in bottom corners, thus :—18. 43.

These stamps are entirely fictitious, and manufactured at Zurich. No stamps were issued in Switzerland till 1850. There were two essays of 1843 made, but they differ considerably from the stamps of the 1850 issue. As probably only two specimens were printed, collectors are not likely to fall in with them, so that an accurate description is not necessary.

Suffice it to say, that the 4 rappen has the words "4 rappen, Local Taxe," printed in an oval round the figure 4, and that the 6 rappen is larger than that of the 1850 issue, and has a very much more intricate background.

1850. 4 rappen, Local Taxe.

Genuine.	*Forged.*
Words "Local-Taxe" joined by hyphen.	There is no hyphen between the words "Local Taxe."
The triangle at right hand end of uppermost horizontal (or cross) stroke of figure 4 is composed of almost straight lines.	In the triangle at right hand end of uppermost horizontal stroke of figure 4, the line nearest to the upright stroke of the figure is strongly concave.
The top of the figure 4, where the line goes towards the left hand bottom corner, is in a line with the left hand line of the upright stroke of the figure. The four corner squares are not much darker than the rest of the stamp. All the lines are of the same colour, giving the stamp rather a dull appearance.	The top of the figure 4, where the line goes towards the left hand bottom corner, projects over the left-hand line of the upright stroke of the figure. The four corner squares are very black, and stand out strongly. The whole stamp is much clearer and brighter; the little semi-circles and ornaments in the border stand out, being much darker than the other lines.

6 rappen, Cantonal-Taxe.

Genuine.	*Forged.*
The words "Cantonal-Taxe" are joined by a hyphen.	There is no hyphen between the words "Cantonal Taxe."
The border is composed of three thin black lines. The middle stroke of the three little black ones, forming the ornaments between the semi-circles in the border, touches the line nearest to the edge.	The border is composed of four thin lines. The middle stroke of the three little black ones, forming the ornaments between the semi-circles in the border, touches the second line from the edge.
The oval (or circle) at the top of figure 6 does not touch the body of the figure.	The oval (or circle) at the top of figure 6 touches the body of the figure.
Each diagonal row of thin black lines (four in each row), is separated from the other by a broad, well defined white space.	The diagonal rows are so close that the white space is hardly noticed.

Both the genuine 4 and 6 rappen are printed on greyish-white unglazed paper. The forged ones are on glazed paper, with the slightest blue tinge.

It should be observed that there are two distinct varieties of both the genuine 4 and 6. In one of the 4's, the black shading on the figure is thicker, the figure is shorter, and the side of the triangle more concave than in the other. Of the 6's, one has the ball at the top of the 6, an oval; the other has it a circle, and a few minor differences will be found on minute examination.

We do not consider these varieties to be different, the differences being too trifling, and arising merely from two dies having been made, but we give this information to prevent our readers thinking, if, for example, they get a 6 with an oval at the top, and one with a circle, that one must be a forgery.

VIII. WINTERTHUR (Canton of Zurich).

1850. Small rectangle. Orts Post.—Post Locale, 2½ rp.

Genuine.	*Forged.*
The red lines on the scroll are thin and close to each other.	The red lines on the scroll are thicker and further apart.
After the word "Post" there is a full stop.	There is no stop after the word "Post."
The horn is bound to the circle enclosing the cross on the left-hand side by a double line.	There is no double line binding the horn to the circle.
The rim at the mouth of the horn is equally thick throughout.	The rim at the mouth of the horn is much thicker on the left side than on the right.
The rope holding up the cross is composed of eight circles on each side.	The rope holding up the cross is composed of six circles on each side.

Of this stamp there are likewise two varieties, one having the horn longer and thinner than the other.

PART II.

STAMPS WHICH NEVER EXISTED, BUT ARE MANUFACTURED BY THE FORGERS.

I. Stamps, of which the Dies were made by the Forgers.
II. Genuine Stamps changed in Colour.

The first head contains only five stamps, of which the Caprera 1 scudo, Bavaria black, 3 kreuzer, and Geneva 10 c. Cantonal, are all more or less imitations of other stamps, but which have all some distinguishing features. The Caprera, for example, is something like the Tuscan; the Bavarian is like the usual ones in most respects, and so on. These stamps will therefore be found under their respective heads in Part I., for as they belong equally to Parts I. and II., we have considered it preferable to describe them in Part I.

The other two stamps belonging solely to this head are the Turkish. We have never had an opportunity of examining these forgeries, but the following are the descriptions we meet with:—6 truzi, olive, crescent and star; 3 mara, red, golden fleece, with letters J. E. below. When these were made, Turkey had not issued stamps, so that they are purely imaginary.

The second head comprises a rather large class of stamps. The majority are those changed in colour by chemical agency, comparatively common stamps serving for this purpose; the others are those Baden which have been altered in price. They are described in alphabetical order, with those changed in colour.

From obvious reasons we have refrained from giving particulars of the processes by which these changes are effected, but, with the most important of these stamps, we give some reasons why they should not be acknowledged as genuine. It will be seen the following are the principal changes:—

Blue to black,
Pink to white or drab,
Green to blue or yellow.

AUSTRIA.

9 krz., arms blue, changed to *green*.

1858.—K. K. Zeitungs Stempel, lavender, changed to *dirty white* (or no colour at all).

BADEN.

1855.—9 krz., pink changed to *white;* 6 krz., yellow to black, by being saturated in ink.

The 6 krz. yellow, 6 green, 9 pink, and the above 9 white, are altered into 9 yellow, 9 green, 6 pink, and 6 white. This is done very ingeniously. The centre circle containing the figure is neatly cut out, turned upside down, and fastened in again by a piece of paper at back. There being nothing in the shape of the figures to betray the change, these stamps met with a good circulation. They originate, we believe, in Leipsic. If one of them is immersed in warm water for a few minutes, the gum will be dissolved, and the centre will fall out.

BAVARIA.

9 krz., green changed to *pale lemon*.

We do not know how this is made (except by one very complicated process, which is not likely to have been the one), but that it is false there can be no doubt, for if the Bavarian Post Office had intended to issue a *yellow* 9 krz., they would have printed it in chrome yellow, as the old 18 k. was, and the present 1 k. now is.

BREMEN.

1855.—5 grote white, and 7 grote pearl grey.

These are the pink and yellow stamps changed.

BRUNSWICK.

1854.—3 sgr., pink to *pale brown.*

We have no proof that this is forged, but the colour is so very dingy, hardly being any colour at all, and the postmarks are so faint, that we can only conclude the colour has been changed from pink to a pale brownish hue by some chemical.

CANADA.

1856.—1½ c. cy., green to *blue.* 1860.—12½c., green to *blue,* and to *black.*

There may have been essays struck from these dies in blue ink, or in black, as mentioned in Mount Brown's catalogue, but all the blue we have seen were made from the green 12½c. by immersion in acid, and the probability is, therefore, that all these blue and black "packet postages" are false.

FRANCE.

1854.—5 cents, blue.

This is the green 5 cents changed.

FRENCH WEST INDIAN POSSESSIONS.

10c. orange, 20 deep indigo.

These are the common French stamps soaked in some coloured solution to give them a tinted ground.

GERMANY, South (Thurn and Taxis).

1860.—1 krz., green to *blue.*

GREAT BRITAIN.

2d. two letters; blue to *black*.

GREECE.

20 lepta, blue to *black*.

There may have been a black essay of this stamp (as mentioned by Mount Brown), but as black ones are made so easily from the blue 20, collectors should be very careful that they do not have one of these latter palmed upon them as an essay, should such a black one really exist.

HANOVER.

1851.—1 gute gr., green to *blue*.

This stamp is mentioned in most catalogues. It is the most important of the changed stamps, and one of those which have been made longest. There are many reasons why the blue 1 gute gr. should not be acknowledged as genuine, apart from the fact that it is so easily made from the green one of the 1851 issue. One reason is, that the blue is such a different shade from that of the 1851 $\frac{1}{15}$ thaler, that it is not likely to have come from the same source. It may be said that the colour is no criterion to go by, seeing that the Hanoverian series of stamps has, in the issue of 1851, *two shades* of $\frac{1}{15}$, a lilac, and a deep blue, and also a $\frac{1}{30}$, dark carmine, and $\frac{1}{30}$ pink. Then again, Saxony, in 1851, had a dark and a light blue 2 groschen. In these cases the two shades are distinct, but then each of them is bright and clear, whilst in the blue 1 gute gr. Hanover, the colour has a *hard* look about it, though excessively clear; it is rather more slate coloured than blue, and it is the very shade obtained by immersion in acid. Again, various gentlemen have more than once obtained sets of the Hanoverian direct from the Government, but no blue 1 gute gr. was there.

1851.—$\frac{1}{15}$ thaler, blue, changed to *white*.

NEW BRUNSWICK.

1861. 5 cents green, changed to blue.

NEW ZEALAND.

1d. dark brown, 1s. dark brown.

Many people who have received these stamps from letters "saved from the wreck of the Colombo," doubtless imagine them to be new kinds. It is the salt water that has changed them, as can easily be noticed by applying them to the tongue, when the salt water is instantly tasted. The 1d. Victoria is also found black, from the same cause.

NORWAY.

1856. 3 sk. lilac, changed to a deep *dull purple* by dye.

NOVA SCOTIA.

1860. 1 cent black to *green*.

This is called an essay by Moens. If it ever existed, it must have been a forgery.

OLDENBURG.

1851. $\frac{1}{3}$ silbgr, green to *yellow*.
1858. $\frac{1}{3}$ groschen do. to *do*.
2 groschen red to *white*.

This last is called an essay by many, but it does not seem to exist, except in forgeries.

PRUSSIA.

1858. 4 pfennige green to *blue*.
1 silbgr pink to *white*.
2 sgr. blue to *drab*.
3 sgr. yellow to *light brown* or *grey*.

These four are sometimes sold by continental dealers as the first stamps used in Prussia.

1850. 2 sgr. blue to *drab*.

SAXONY.

1851. 1 neugr pink to *white*.
3 ngr. yellow to *deep crimson* by some dye.
3 ngr. yellow to *white*.

SWITZERLAND.

Rayon II. 10 rappen, yellow to *slate colour*.

UNITED STATES.

1857. 1 c. blue, 3 c. red, 5 c. brown, 10 c. green, 12 c. black, on white paper, changed to a *dark olive* colour, by immersion in colouring matter.
10 cent green to *blue*.

VICTORIA.

6d. blue, Queen on throne, to *black.*

There may have been a black essay of this stamp, but we have noticed that, by proper management, a very dark blue-black one may be obtained, so dark as to pass for black. This sort is the one most likely to be met with, so collectors should be careful with them.

WURTEMBERG.

1850. 9 krz. rose changed to *white.*
1850. 6 krz. green to *blue.*

NOTE —Seeing that the green 6 can be altered to blue so readily, we would advise collectors to "fight shy" of blue 6 krz. (1850 pattern), which may be sent them as essays. We have never seen one of these essays, but, on receiving one, we should not accept it readily, unless it came from a perfectly safe source.

PART III.

STAMPS NEVER INTENDED AS FORGERIES, BUT WHICH HAVE BEEN ACKNOWLEDGED AS REAL, THROUGH SOME MISCONCEPTION.

There are seventy-one of these, but forty-seven are the so-called complementary stamps of Austria. Some are trade labels, some are satires on the English design of 1840, some are receipt stamps, one is an advertisement, and others bill stamps. There is so little of interest in these, that we will proceed upon them at once.

AUSTRIA.

It does not seem that these "complementary labels" were ever intended for any further purpose than to fill up the proper number or complement of stamps on a sheet, which (Moens tells us), is sixty, in eight rows, the space over that being filled up by crosses of the same colour as the stamp. It seems there are no less than forty-seven of them, as follows :—

1850. St Andrew's Cross, in colour on a white ground, orange, yellow, black, red, brown, and blue, to match the 1850 stamp (with the arms) of those colours.
1858. White cross, on a coloured ground of orange, yellow, black, green, red, brown, and blue, to match the stamps of this issue with the head.

Then these last are found with each colour having in addition either one, two, three, or four dots in relief,—making *twenty-eight* sorts more. Those on the sheets of stamps now used have the cross in white relief, and the whole stamp has a white border and perforated edges: colours yellow, black, green, red, brown, and blue.

BAVARIA.

1851 and 1862. The whole issue is also found in black on coloured paper. These are the so-called "Timbres d'instruction." They are stuck on the outside of the packets sent to the postmasters, to let them know what kind is enclosed.

BRUNSWICK.

Horn and horse in oval, with words Post-schein above, and value below.
6 pf. red, lake.
½ g. gr. red.

Stamps impressed on the receipts given for registered letters at the Post Office; they are not used for postal purposes.

DENMARK.

Black impression, design of the Danish stamp, but with the figure 3 in centre, and word Thiele at sides.

A Copenhagen printer, of the name of Thiele, advertised in some Danish publication. His form of advertisement was an envelope directed to himself, having engraved in the corner allotted to the stamp the above design; the label was of course printed on the paper, *i.e.* was not first struck and then fastened to the advertisement with gum as a real stamp would have been.

FRANCE.

Small head of the emperor printed on a label about the size of a ¼ sch. Mecklenburg; also the same size as the usual labels, but without words. The colours are various. These are trade labels, found on packets of French confectionaries. They *never* had any other meaning.

GREAT BRITAIN.

Mulready's design for the 1d. and 2d. envelopes issued in 1840, from their peculiar appearance, gave rise to many satirical imitations, having, however, no power of franking their contents without the aid of a 1d. stamp. These would not have needed notice here, only Dr Gray giving them in the first edition of his catalogue, may tend to mislead beginners, so we will just mention them in the same order that he does.

Fox's comic envelope by John Leech, 1840. Rejected designs for the postage envelope, nos. 1, 2, 3, 4, 5, and 6, 1840. Paul Pry's envelope by John Leech, engraved by W. J. Linton.

We need say no more, so pass on to

ICELAND.

These so-called stamps are also trade labels, the design is a bear in a shield, with the inscription "Vulnere" below, the colours are various. It denotes the presence of bear's grease in packages.

JAMAICA.

Arms, two men holding a shield with an inscription, coloured impression.
1½d. blue, 3d. purple.

These are bill stamps used in Jamaica.

OCEAN POSTAGE.

Moens, in his "Falsifications," mentions six sorts of these envelopes, we have only seen the three first: They all of them bear emblematical designs of "Peace and Plenty," which the promoters of the Ocean Penny Postage Scheme thought would accrue from the adoption of their favourite plan. They have no official origin, being issued by private individuals, enthusiasts on the subject. They were *never* intended as envelope stamps for postal purposes, but merely as a sort of advertisement to draw attention to the scheme of a universal penny postage between England and all her colonies. The first sort described has printed in the *left* hand upper corner, a head of Mercury in the form of a stamp, with the words "Ocean Postage" on it. That this never could have been intended to frank the letter to its destination, is fully shewn by the fact that in the *right* hand upper corner, there is a blank space left for the stamp of the country whence the letter comes. All these envelopes that we have seen, have had the old blue 6d. South Australian stamp there.

1st, Railway, &c., along the top of *Envelope*; at side, ships unlading, and various devices emblematical of commercial and agricultural prosperity. Inscription on the envelope, "Britain! from thee, the world expects an Ocean Penny Postage, to make her children one fraternity."

2d, Vessel under full sail, inscription, "The world awaits Great Britain's greatest gift, an Ocean Penny Postage—to make home everywhere, and all nations neighbours."

3d, Sailor with flag, &c., inscription, "Ocean Penny Postage," and "Britain! bestow this boon; and thou in blessing blest, will link all lands with thee in trade and peace."

The three next sorts we have had no opportunity of examining, but the descriptions we meet with are somewhat to the following effect:—

4th, Allegorical design of Britain and the lion distributing freedom, on the left hand are drawn negroes under various tortures; the figure of Britain is under the shadow of a flag, bearing the inscription, "God hath made of one blood all the nations of men."

5th, Two large Cornucopiæ forming a space in the centre, for the direction on the envelope; on the left hand side the prophecy from Isaiah xi. 6. with suitable design; to the right that from Isaiah ii. 4. with drawing to match. The inscription is, "Nation shall not lift up sword against nation, neither shall they learn war any more."

6th, Design showing universal peace and commerce, a soldier and artizan fraternizing; the Angel of peace, etc., etc. Inscription, "Arbitration for war, universal brotherhood, freedom of commerce."

Doubtless, there are many more of these envelopes, but these six are all that we can find noticed. No one, after reading the inscriptions and noticing the designs, could suppose they were of any use for prepaying letters as envelope stamps are, nor would one think they ever had any further intention than to bring the universal system of Ocean Penny Postage into repute and notice.

SWITZERLAND.

I. BERNE.

Bear in a shield, with a crown below, inscription, "Canton Berne," coloured impression, rectangular.

10 rap. yellow, 3 rap. blue.

These are bill or receipt stamps.

II. GENEVA.

Man with spear, leaning on a shield with a cross in the centre, date given "Sept. 1857," coloured impression, rectangular. Various values and colours.

These are bill or receipt stamps.

III. ZURICH

Mercury seated. Various values.

These are all bill or receipt stamps.

ADDENDA.

There are two stamps, possibly misprints, or else of which only a very few were made, about which nothing certain is known.

These are the 49 Modena and the 3 Naples. There was a 9 Modena, so that possibly the Post Office may have intended to issue a 49, for several specimens are known.

We have only seen or heard of one 3 Naples. It is like the 5 in all respects, but the figure is quite perfect.

The Paraguay Stamps are a *vexata quæstio.* Mount Brown and Moens call them Essays; Laplante and Dr Gray mention 3 Stamps as being used there.

We possess a most beautiful specimen of the magenta one, *obliterated* by means of dots, diamond shaped like the French, with the letters "L. P." in the middle. We have also had sent us a rather fainter specimen of the same stamp, unused, which had some considerable points of difference from ours. We subjoin a description of both, and shall be happy to learn something definite and positive about them.

Obliterated Specimen.	*Unobliterated Specimen.*
Bright, clear magenta, extremely well executed.	Much fainter, and not so well executed; it looks coarser.
All the lines are sharp and thin.	The lines are blotchy.
The ornament in the oval surrounding the lion is very thin and neat.	The ornament in the oval surrounding the lion is thick.
The cap of liberty is not shaded.	The cap of liberty is shaded.
The lion is not shaded.	The lion is shaded.
The mane on the right hand side is quite white.	The mane on the right is quite pink.
The tail is thin, with pointed tip, which is thicker than the rest of the tail.	The tail is thicker, more perpendicular, and the tip thinner in proportion, and round.

Of the 1853 British Guiana issue, there are two varieties, one has the figures 1. 8. 5. 3. enclosed by a white border, and the other merely by a line, and there is a little difference in the ornaments.

The following is a table of the prices of some forged stamps, and the prices they fetch when genuine. There are some of them, the prices of which, when forged, we do not know. These we have, of course, left blank.

	Forged.	*Genuine.*
Argentine Confederation,........	...	used 1s. 6d.—2s. unused 2s.—3s.
Confederate States,................	6d.—1s.	each fetches several shillings.
Denmark (Essays),................	1s. 6d.—2s.	2s. 6d.—3s. 6d.
Modena 9 B. G. and 1 lira,.......	unused and used, 1s.—1s. 6d.	unused, priceless. used, 3s.—4s.
Modena, the other eagles,..........	1s.—1s. 6d.	used, 1s. 6d.—2s.
Tassa Gazzette...........	1s. 6d.	

	Forged.	*Genuine.*
Provisional Government, 15-80,	1s. 6d.—2s.	priceless.
The others, ...	1s. 6d.—2s.	2s.
Parma, Provisional Government,	unused, 1s.—1s. 6d.	used 1s. 6d.—2s. unused, priceless.
Romagna, ., ...	unused or used, 1s.—1s. 6d.	used 2s.—3s. 6d. unused 5s.
Sandwich Islands. The forged and genuine are sold at about the same price, 2s.—2s. 6d.		
Spain, 1 cuarto bronze, ...		priceless.
Switzerland.		
Basle, ...	1s.—1s. 6d.	2s. 6d.—3s.
Geneva, Port Local, ...	1s.—1s. 6d.	3s—4s.
... Port Cantonal, ...	1s.—1s. 6d.	2s.—3s.
Neuchâtel, ...	1s.—1s. 6d.	5s.
Vaud, ...	1s.—1s. 6d.	2s. 6d.—3s.
Zurich, ...	1s.—1s. 6d.	2s.—2s. 6d.
Orts Post, ...	9d.	9d.
Poste Locale, ...	9d.	1s. 6d.
Winterthur, ...	1s.—1s. 6d.	2s. 6d.
Naples, ½ t. blue cross, ...	1s.—2s.	used 3s. 6d. unused priceless.
... ... arms, ...	1s.—2s.	used 5s. unused priceless.

HOW TO DETECT

FORGED STAMPS.

BY

THOMAS DALSTON.

CONTAINING ACCURATE AND
COMPREHENSIVE DESCRIPTIONS OF ALL FORGED AND
FICTITIOUS STAMPS.

PRICE ONE SHILLING, POST FREE 13 STAMPS.

Gateshead:
PRINTED AND PUBLISHED BY R. CHAMBERS, 115, HIGH STREET.

1865.

CONTENTS

FICTITIOUS STAMPS.

STAMPS NEVER INTENDED FOR POSTAL USE.

STAMPS WHICH HAVE BEEN CHANGED IN COLOUR BY CHEMICALS.

INTRODUCTION

More than twenty-four years ago the first Postage Stamp was issued in England. Formerly the postage of letters was paid in money, either before posting or on delivery; but now it is done by merely affixing a postage stamp. It was indeed a great mind that originated this method of prepaying postage, which for simplicity and economy, both of money and time, cannot be equalled. England was the first country which commenced the postage stamp system, and Sir Rowland Hill deservedly claims credit for its introduction. After England, Zurich appears to have adopted the new system, and a few years later, Belgium and the French Republic issued stamps. The very rare Madrid local stamps, bearing the arms of that city printed in bronze, was also issued at the same time. Another year later, and the Spanish, Baden, Wurtemburg, Prussian, and Thurn und Taxis stamps appeared, and not long after commenced the gradual and rapid adoption of the system in almost all the other continental states, and in fact in nearly every part of the civilized world.

The interesting and instructive amusement of collecting postage stamps did not commence until about four or five years ago, when the great number of stamps that had been issued in different countries, attracted a little attention; but now, the number of collectors in England alone may be counted by hundreds, whilst in France, Germany, Italy, and America, the pursuit is gradually extending

It is quite unnecessary here to expiate upon the pleasure or information to be derived from the study and collection of stamps, because it is presumed that all who refer to this small volume have already felt some taste and fondness for the pursuit. The non-collector who demands an explanation of the use of the study of stamps, I must refer to the introduction in Dr. Grey's Catalogue, which, I have no doubt, will convince the most averse non-collector, that there is some instruction in stamp collecting, and I can only add that the pursuit is so congenial to the taste, instructing and elevating to the mind, and so productive of good, that all collectors, become enthusiastic in the pursuit.

A postage stamp in addition to its use in prepaying letters, is a species of paper money, circulated by the state, which represents a fixed amount of sterling currency, and is negotiable through the Post-office, as a national bank is held responsible for the notes issued; and in order to prevent forgers from imitating them, the best artists and engravers are procured to design and execute stamps, which will at once comprise beautiful with intricate engravings, and thus in some degree render the efforts of forgers to imitate very difficult, if not impossible. There have been more than 2300 postage stamps issued in all parts of the world, and out of that number about 500 have been forged, yet I do not know of hardly any forgeries that have been executed for the express purpose of prepaying postage, and thus swindling the respective governments. The first forgeries appear to have been executed about three years and a half ago; indeed, I do not know of any that were executed prior to that time. The forgers mostly imitate old obsolete stamps, which are invariably simple in design, and commanding high prices; in fact, I have known instances of used specimens having sold for the great sum of one sovereign. There are, however, considerable quantities of stamps forged that are in present use, and some are exceedingly close imitations, and could easily pass as genuine in their respective countries, if they were not closely observed, and compared with undoubtedly genuine specimens.

I saw in a French paper, not long ago, that a vessel, laden with powder, and bound for Liberia, blew up, and on looking over the *debris*, a large packet of Liberian stamps, unobliterated,* directed to the English Consul, were found. A collector being present, discovered that they were Hamburg forgeries. The paragraph concluded by saying that without doubt they were intended to deceive the government, and that it was probable the negroes of Liberia had been thus imposed upon for a long time. This therefore shows that imitations which are sufficiently well executed to pass as genuine in the country of which its stamps are imitated, must needs deceive collectors, without they exercise great care, and as they cannot always obtain the loan of genuine specimens to compare with, it is the object of the present volume to fill up that deficiency, by supplying to each possessor of a postage stamp collection, a ready and sure mode of ascertaining whether the stamps are genuine or not, which can not be done by any work hitherto published. The method of comparing with genuine stamps is, on consideration, perfectly impracticable, for forgeries, owing to the small price for which they can be obtained, have now so large a circulation, that it is perfectly unsafe to trust to this method. I have known instances where two persons have had two different forgeries, and of course have been much puzzled to know which was genuine. In many instances there are two different forgeries of

* The Liberian stamps usually sold to collectors are neatly post-marked.

one stamp, in some three, and all these being different in workmanship, I have had to describe separately; so it will be seen I have had no easy task in bringing to light all the forgeries. This book also provides the general reader with a tolerably compact account of all the forgeries, and although my aim has been throughout to make the descriptions as concise and comprehensive as possible, yet I have at the same time described the genuine in such a manner, that if at any future time there should be more, and of course in some degree different imitations of the same stamp issued, the descriptions will serve to detect them.

A necessary, but not an agreeable part of my labour is to detect and point out the mistakes and errors of my predecessors. The English translation of Moens "*Falsification*" is utterly unfit for reliance, and ought not to be depended upon. In some of his descriptions he neither properly describes the genuine or the forgery; in fact, some appear to have been taken from two different forgeries. The reader will already be aware that there are sometimes several forgeries of some particular stamps. These descriptions have therefore destroyed all confidence in the work. Mr. Pemberton, in "*Forged Stamps, how to detect them,*" is perfectly honest, and any inaccuracies which may occur in his work—and they are very few—must be attributed to error, not to design. In his first edition (the second has not yet come out) he only occupies about 15 pages with real forgeries. The rest of the book is composed of fictitious stamps, and stamps the colours of which are changed by chemicals, most of which, also, are fictitious, and out of nearly 500 forgeries, he has only described about 60 of them. I think it is useless devoting so much space to fictitious stamps; but as there are a great quantity in the market, I have appended a list of all the fictitious stamps that have been issued, and the stamps that have been changed in colour by chemicals, but, as it is very probable there may be more fictitious stamps issued, I would caution collectors not to purchase any stamps as rare that are not mentioned in the best catalogues, or any that are new which are not mentioned in the "*Stamp Collector's Magazine,*" "*Stamp Collector's Miscellany,*" or "*Stamp Collector's Examiner,*" all of which publish descriptions of new issues as soon as it is possible for dealers to get them.

The principal persons who forge stamps reside on the Continent. Spiro Brothers of Hamburg, have produced the most, and some of them are exceedingly well executed, amongst which are the Bergedorf, British Guiana, Finland, Geneva, Greece, Hamburg, Liberia, Old Lubeck, New Granada, Nicaragua, Pony Express, Schleswig, Saxony, Western Australia, and many others. All that I have seen are post-marked—most of them are perforated —and the Schleswig $1\frac{1}{4}$ sch., has even the water mark in the paper. Indeed, the above dealers have made quite a trade of it, and a very profitable trade too. There is a dealer in Zurich who sells good imitations of the Swiss Canton stamps, and there is another in Brussels whose forgeries are well executed, and widely circulated. Glasgow has turned out many *fac-similes*, but about all of them are inferior to the above in execution. I also find that there has been different forgeries executed in London, Manchester, and Newcastle, but they are only inferior imitations. I have also received some pretty good forgeries from New York, but the only passable ones are those sent from the Continent.

In concluding this brief introduction, I must thank the various gentlemen who have kindly sent me doubtful stamps on inspection, and who have also given me assistance in the compilation of this small, but, it is hoped, useful book; amongst the latter I must include Mr. D. Dean, editor and publisher of the "*Stamp Collector's Miscellany*," who has rendered me great assistance. I shall be very glad to give my opinion upon any doubtful stamp which may be sent me on inspection.

THOS. DALSTON,

MARKET PLACE,

April, 1865. BARNARD CASTLE.

HOW TO DETECT FORGED STAMPS.

ANTIGUA.

Name, Head of Queen Victoria, 1d. red.

This is a very poor imitation. The outline of the face, however, is very correct; but on a close examination of the back-ground, it will be perceived that instead of very fine and minute engraving, it is composed of smudged dots.

ARGENTINE CONFEDERATION.

1861 *issue.—Name* ARGENTINE CONFE^{ON}., *design rising sun with cap of Liberty, coloured impression on white paper, 2c. red, 5c. green, 10c. blue.*

There are several separate and distinct forgeries of this set of stamps, which slightly differ in execution, so that I append separate descriptions. In the two first descriptions, it will be seen I have mentioned, that in the genuine 5 centav there is a dot after 2, but in the 10 c. and 15 c. there is no dot after 10 or 15, whilst in the forgery all three have dots after numeral of value. This may be accounted for in the following manner:—most forgers of stamps when about to engrave a set of stamps in which the design of all of them is the same, except some trifling thing which has escaped notice, choose any genuine stamp of that set they have at hand, and engrave the whole set therefrom, referring to a catalogue for information as to colour, &c.; or it may be, having the stamp to buy for the engraver, they have selected the cheapest. Further on it will be seen that this mistake has often occurred when forging a set of stamps, the design of which is in all of them the same.

No. 1 FORGERY.

GENUINE.	FORGED.
The hands hold a small staff, at the top of which is a cap of Liberty.	The staff and cap of Liberty are both left out; probably the engraver had a copy with that part of the stamp covered by the obliterating mark.
The glory round the head is not so thick as that near the border.	The glory round the head is of the same thickness throughout.
There is a dot after 5 in the 5 centav stamp, but not in the 10 c. and 15 c.	There is a dot after the numeral of value in all three stamps.

No. 2 FORGERY.

Genuine. The cap of Liberty is in most cases very much smeared.

Forged. The cap of Liberty is very clear, even clearer than in the genuine.

Genuine. The G of Argentine is very clumsy, and not at all like the C of Confeon.

Forged. The G of Argentine is almost exactly like the C of Confeon.

Genuine. The top dash of the two dashes under Confeon is the same length as the bottom one.

Forged. The top dash is much shorter than the bottom one.

Genuine. The oval containing staff, cap of Liberty, &c., touches the border of the stamp at the right and left sides.

Forged. The oval does not touch the border.

Genuine. There is a dot after the 5 of 5 centav, but not after the 10 or 15 c.

Forged. There is a dot after figure of value in all the set.

No. 3 FORGERY.

Genuine. The E of Confeon is the same size as the other letters of that word, excepting O N.

Forged. The E is much larger than the other letters of that word.

Genuine. The G of Argentina does not touch the E.

Forged. The G does touch the E.

Genuine. The glory round the head is not thick.

Forged. The glory round the head is thick.

The last described forgery is decidedly the best executed of the lot, but it may be remembered that the whole of the forged Argentine Confederation stamps are too bright in colour.

ARGENTINE REPUBLIC.

Name, 5 centavos, red.

This is a badly executed imitation; the lettering of inscription is very bad and irregular, in some places smudged; in the genuine, however, the inscription is very clear and well defined. The whole appearance of the stamp is very bad, and it looks as if it had been printed as cheaply as possible.

AUSTRIA.

1855.—Newspaper Labels.—*Arms, inscription "Kais Kon Zeitungs stempel;" coloured imp. square* 1 *kr. black,* 2 *kr. green, and red brown.*

1858.—*Same design as last,* 1 *kr. blue,* 2 *kr. brown, and* 4 *kr. red brown.*

There are numerous differences between the genuine and forgeries in the above stamps, but the undermentioned will suffice. The genuine stamps are wood engravings, whilst the forgeries are lithographed.

Genuine. The letters and eagle are clear.

Forged. The letters and eagle are not clear.

Genuine. In each corner there is a round ornament, and on two sides of it is a kite-shaped ornament; the latter does not touch the former.

Forged. The round ornaments are smudgy, and they touch the kite-shaped ones.

1857.—*Head of Mercury to left, blue, yellow, and pink.*

GENUINE.	FORGED.
The letters of inscription are pretty regular, and all are about the same thickness throughout.	The letters of inscription are not all same size, and are badly executed.
The letter T in stempel at bottom is very clear and well shaped.	The letter T in stempel at bottom is very badly defined; the left side of the top part of it is less than the other side.
The ornaments in all four corners are almost all like each other.	There is great differences between the four ornaments in the four corners.

BADEN.

1850.—1 *kreuzer buff.*

In the forgery the letters of inscription are rather irregular, but in the genuine they are very regular. The ornaments at top and bottom of the inscription at sides, are all separate at the bottom; in the forgery, they however, touch one another at the bottom in the genuine.

1862.—18 *kr. green and* 30 *kr. orange.*

GENUINE.	FORGED.
The corner ornaments are very clear and finely engraved, and on comparison with the present issue 1 kr. black stamp (which is comparatively common), they will be found to be alike.	The corner ornaments are very irregular, and differ very much with the 1 kr. black.
The dots of the shield are very regular, all nearly of the same size, and in straight rows.	The dots on the shield are very irregular, and are scattered about here and there.

UNPAID LETTER LABELS.—*Inscription: "Land-Post Porto Marke," figure indicating value, black impression on yellow paper,* 1 *kreuzer,* 3 *kr.,* 12 *kr.*

GENUINE.	FORGED.
The letter S in "Land Post" is very regular.	The letters in "Land Post" are very irregular.
The hyphen between Land and Post is below the centre of the letter P.	The hyphen is almost at the centre of P.
The colour of the paper is a darkish yellow.	The colour of the paper is very light yellow.

Most of the above genuine stamps are perforated, but the above forgeries are not. I have, however, seen a badly perforated 1 kr, which was also very badly executed.

ENVELOPE, 3 *kr. blue.*

In the forgery the head is badly embossed, and the parting of the hair is invisible; it is also printed on thicker paper than the genuine. Altogether it is well printed, but the engraving has been badly done. The inscription across the envelope, in the forgery, is printed in roughly formed letters, the colour being lemon instead of orange. The imitation appears to be lithographed, but the genuine is die printed.

BAVARIA.

1849.—*Inscription "Bayern Franco riu Kreuzer," large figure indicating value in a square,* 1 *kr. black.*

GENUINE.	FORGED.
The ornamentation of the large figure 1 is very clear.	The ornamentation of the large figure is much coarser than the genuine.
The large figure is not particularly distinct and clear at first sight.	The large figure is very perceptible.
The ornamentation in the back-ground is very fine and clear when closely observed.	The ornamentation is rather coarse, and can be distinctly traced without much looking at.
The paper on which it is printed is not exactly white and the ink is not shiny.	The paper is very white and the ink is rather shiny.

There are also photographs of this valuable stamp in the market which are of course correct in every detail; and if any of our readers are suspicious of the above stamp, or, in fact, of any other black stamp or essay whatever, which they may think is photographed, they may easily detect it by applying cyanuret of potassa (a chemical which may be obtained at any druggists) to the face of the engraving. If photographed it will instantly remove the impression, leaving the paper white; whereas if the stamp has been printed in the usual way, it will not injure it in the least.

1862. UNPAID LETTER LABEL.—*Black impression on white paper,* 3 *kreuzer.*

This forgery is printed in shiny ink, and is altogether a poor imitation. The execution is in all respects bad, and when compared with the other adhesive stamps of the same country may be easily detected.

BARBADOES.

Name, coloured impression on blue paper, value not indicated, red, blue, and green.

These three stamps are forged, and are well designed, but they are very badly printed, and are all lithographed. They are also easily recognizable by the smaller print of the characters.

BERGEDORF.

1861.—*Name, black impression on coloured paper* ½ *sch. violet,* 3 *sch. rose.*

GENUINE.	FORGED.
The number of small circles in the large ring round the arms in both the above stamps is 55.	The number of small circles in the ½ sch. is 46, and in the 3 sch. is 52.

There are also forgeries of the ½, 3, and 4 sch. of the present issue. The ½ and 3 sch. are printed from the same dies as the above, so that the above description will suffice. The forged 4 sch. has 55 small circles round the arms.

BRAZIL.

All the first issue and the 10, 30, and 60 reis of the second issue are forged. They are all however badly imitated, especially the second issue, where the forger has omitted to shade the figures, and instead of engine turned lines of dots in the background, there is only smudged dots.

BREMEN.

1855.—*Black impression on blue paper,* 3 *grote.*

Genuine.	Forged.
The A of Stadt is exactly like the A of AMT.	The A of Stadt is longer and unlike the A of AMT.
Both the letters T of Stadt are alike.	The first T of Stadt is much larger than the other.
The D of Stadt is flat on the top.	The D of Stadt is round on the top.
The letters of Stadt Post Amt are of a uniform size.	The letters of Stadt Post Amt are very irregular in size.

1855.—*Green impression on white paper,* 5 *s. gr.*

Genuine.	Forged.
On a careful examination of the 5 s. gr, it will be perceived that almost half a dozen of the thin background lines run through the border, half way down the 5, the same number running through the border to the top of the S, and on the outside of the gr. will be found some very short strokes.	The 5 s. gr. is quite plain, and there is nothing of the kind on it as mentioned opposite.
The top part of the outside of the oval containing the key does not touch the line holding the key.	The top part of the ornament touches the line.

1863.—2 *grote, orange.*

Genuine.	Forged.
The outside of the ornamentation enclosing Bremen and Zwie Grote consists of round lines, very regular, and never pointed.	The outside of the ornamentation is irregular and in many cases pointed.
The above-mentioned ornamentation touches the inside line enclosing the word Stadt.	The ornamentation does not touch the line.

1855.—5 *grote, rose, black impression.*

Genuine.	Forged.
The ornaments at corners at the outside of the line are regular and like each other.	The ornaments are much unlike each other.
The M in Marke is like the usual printed capital M,	The last stroke of the M is longer than the other strokes.

1861.—10 *grote, black impression.*

Genuine.	Forged.
The dots outside the oval enclosing key are pretty clear.	The dots are in some parts blotched.
The letters of inscription are firm and neat.	The two E's in Bremen are unlike each other, and the shading of all the letters are rather blotchy.
The figure 0 in 10 at the right side top corner is like the other figures in the other corners.	The figure 0 is badly shaped.

BRITISH GUIANA.

1860.—*Name, ship in full sail to right in garter,* 1 *cent black,* 2 *c. red,* 4 *c. blue,* 8 *c. plush,* 12 *c. grey,* 24 *c. light green.*

Genuine.	Forged,
There is a dot in the centre of each of the two star ornaments upon the garter, which is very clear.	Neither the dot or the ornaments are distinct or clear; in fact, the dot cannot be seen at all.
The two G's in Guiana and Postage are both alike.	The G in Guiana is not so well shaped as the other.
The lines forming the sky are very close together, and not to be traced by the naked eye.	These lines may be easily perceived, and even counted.
They are very nicely printed.	Most of the forgeries are badly printed and have a washy look, which will not easily deceive the experienced collector.

Newspaper Labels with Pearl Bordering.

There appears to be much uncertainty amongst collectors and others, respecting these labels, *i. e.*, which are authentic and which not. All the genuine I have seen have a signature in the centre, mostly in red ink, and invariably blotched. The B in British and the S in Cents, are not on a level with the other letters, being a little lower. The O in Two is like a C, and the U in Guiana touches the top line. I have only seen one set of forgeries, and it is in most cases, I understand, post-marked with four short thick smudgy lines, instead of the letters and figure A. O. 3. I may also state, that in all genuine stamps, the shading in the little circles or pearls forming the border is towards the inside, and the circles are seen with two fine outlines, which gives them the appearance of one thick one.

BRUNSWICK.

1852.—*Name, Braunschweig, arms, value in figures on each side, coloured impression,* 1 *silb. gr. rose,* 2 *s. gr. blue,* 3 *s. gr. vermillion.*

1854.—$\frac{1}{4}$ *s gr. brown,* $\frac{1}{3}$ *s. gr. white,* 1 *s. gr. yellow,* 2 *s. gr. blue,* 3 *s. gr. pink.*

Genuine.	Forged.
The colour of the 3 s. gr. is vermillion.	The colour of the 3 s. gr. is light brown and the colours of the other stamps are rather thin.
The crown in the oval is clear and well defined.	The crown is indistinct.
The inscription is very regular.	The inscription is badly done, and is rather irregular as to size, &c.
The printing is very nice and clear.	The printing is blotchy, especially the shading.

1862.—*Same device, coloured impression,* 3 *silb. gr.*

The forgery is printed in red orange, instead of rose. The letters of the inscription are also uneven. Altogether it is a poor imitation, and is badly printed.

Envelopes.—*Inscription: St. P. Fr. in circle; printed in red with hand stamp on coloured paper, green, white, blue, and yellow.*

These stamps when genuine are so plain and simple in design that it is extremely easy to forge them. The forgeries are wretchedly printed and there is no curl at the bottom of the T.

BUENOS AYRES.

Name, Head of Liberty in a circle, 1 *peso blue, and rose,* 2 *pesos blue.*

Genuine.	Forged.
The letters of Peso are all of equal size.	The letters of Peso gradually diminish in size the P being the largest and the O the smallest.
The top curl of the hair *is* shaded.	The top curl of the hair is *not* shaded.
The letters in the inscription are all well formed.	The letters are in most cases badly formed and irregular in size.

CONFEDERATE STATES OF AMERICA.

1861.—*Name, Bust of Jefferson Davis to right in oval,* 5 *cents blue, and* 5 *c. green.*

Genuine.	Forged.
The background appears almost solid, being composed of very fine close lines.	The lines in the background are wide apart, and very distinct.
The head is some space from the inscription above.	The hair of the head almost touches the letters above.
The inscription is printed in short compact letters.	The letters are thin and rather apart.

Name, Bust of Davis in circle, 5 c. blue.

GENUINE.

In the corners round the head are some stars which do *not* touch the lines outside them.

The engraving is very good, letters rounded and clearly defined.

FORGED.

Most of the outside stars *do* touch the lines.

The engraving is some places deficient, especially shading, and the letters long, thin, and badly printed.

Name, 2 c. green, 10 c. blue and rose, 20 c. green.

These stamps are badly executed, and could not well pass as genuine. I am of opinion that they were not originally intended to cheat collectors, as I have almost always seen them sold in sets and as *fac-similes;* but one dealer sent them to me on inspection as genuine, saying the government having run out of their stamps before they could get fresh ones, had to get a local engraver to execute some, specimens of which he enclosed me. The colours are in all cases very thin and washy in the forgery, and the engraving very bad. Some are printed better than others, but in all cases the stamps are blotched more or less, (that is, in the forgery.) The inscription is also very bad.

NEW ORLEANS.

1861.—*Name, figure indicating value in circle, inscription ; J. C. Riddell. 2 c. red, 2 c. blue.*

GENUINE.

The letters are all regular but rather indistinct.

The printing is altogether rather indistinct and appears to be coarse.

FORGED.

Some of the letters are thin and others thick, but the whole are very distinct.

The printing is very clear and very fine.

5 c. mauve, 5 c. brown

GENUINE.

The letters in the word Post touch the line above them.

The mark between New-Orleans touches the O.

The right hand top ornament is rather shaded.

FORGED.

None of the letters touch the line.

It does not touch the O.

The right hand top ornament is quite clear.

RICHMOND.

Inscription : Richmond Postage, 5 cents, flag in oval, 5 cents green and yellow.

GENUINE.

The ink with which it is printed is not shiny.

The outside line enclosing the whole stamp is very firm and clear throughout.

FORGED.

The ink is shiny.

The outside line is in some parts, especially at corners, very indistinct, and there are several gaps.

NASHVILLE.

1861.—*Name, figure indicating value in oval, 5 cents crimson.*

GENUINE.	FORGED.
The printing is very indistinct and smudged.	The printing is very distinct and clear.
The border is composed of one white line.	The border consists of two white lines one thick and the other thin.
The stars are thick and rather smudged.	The stars are pretty small.

CUBA.

1857.—*Coloured impression on white paper, ½ rl. plata blue, 1 rl. pl. green, 2 rl. pl. green.*

GENUINE.	FORGED.
The execution is good, and all the stamp is clearly printed.	The engraving is in some places bad, and the printing is rather blotchy.
The beads within the central circle are all of one size.	The lower beads are smaller than the upper ones.

COSTA RICA.

1863.—*½ real blue, 2 r. green.*

GENUINE.	FORGED.
The letters RE of Real touch each other.	The letter RE do not touch each other.
The letters of Medio Real are all the same size.	The letters are not all the same size.
The sea behind the mountains on the right side of the left hand mountain, is on a level with that on the left side of the said mountain.	The sea behind the mountains on the right side of the left hand mountain, is much lower than that on the left side.
The letters of Real mostly touch each other.	The letters of Real never touch each other.

DANUBIAN PRINCIPALITIES.

MOLDAVIA.

1854.—54 *paras green,* 81 *par. blue,* 108 *par. rose.*

These three simply designed stamps are very well imitated. The inscription in the forgery is in all three rather irregular. In the 81 par. the ear on the left hand side is lower down than the opposite one. At the wide end of the bugle-horn in the forgery of the 108 par. is 5 strokes to represent shading.

1861.—*Inscription: Porto Scrisorei, coloured impression,* 40 *paras blue,* 80 *par. red.*

Newspaper Label.—*Inscription: Porto Gazette,* 5 *paras black.*

The above three imitations emanate from Glasgow. None of them have got a thin stroke to join the two thick ones of the H together in Hap. The colouring is exceedingly thin and poor, and they are badly printed on nearly transparent paper. In the 5 paras the right hand bulls ear appears not to be finished. In the 40 p. both the right hand ear and horn is thinner than the opposite ones, and the right ear in the 40 p. and also the 80 p. points more to the top corner than the left hand ones.

MOLDO WALLACHIA.

1862.—*Inscription: Franco Scrisorei eagle displayed and bull's head ovor bugle horn,* 30 *par. blue.*

The forgers of this stamp have made a very flagrant error, which will at once detect it, viz:—by omitting the R in Scrisorei. Probably the stamp used by the engraver to copy from was much obliterated about that part.

DENMARK.

1852.—*Inscription; Kgl. Post Frimœrke* 2 *rigsbank skilling blue.*

Genuine.	Forged.
The M in Frimœrke is neatly printed.	The second stroke, *i. e.*, the first thick one in the M is clumsily done, and not so thick as the last stroke.
The mouthpiece of the horn is pointed towards the left hand top corner.	The horn is only slightly curved from the middle to the mouthpiece, and therefore does not point up to the corner.
The mouthpiece end of the horn is very thin.	The end is rather thicker.

Essay.—*Head of Mercury,* 4 *R. B. S.,* (1¼ *sch. c.*)

Essay.—*Head of King,* 8 *R. B, S.,* (2½ *sch. c.*)*; colour brown, on a ground composed of diagonal blue strokes.*

Genuine.	Forged.
The figure 4 in Head of Mercury Stamp is like the *written* figure.	The figure 4 is like the usual *printed* figure.
The wing at the far side of the Mercury's head is higher than the one nearest, so that a narrow piece of the whole length of the wing is perceptible.	There is only a very little of the far side wing to be seen.
The King's ear is only partly to be seen, the top half being covered by the hair.	The King's ear is wholly perceptible.

DUCHY OF SCHLESWIG-HOLSTEIN.

1848.—1 *sch. blue,* 2 *sch. rose.*

There are very good imitations of the above old Provisional Government Stamps, which are well engraved and printed, but they are disfigured with great blotchy postmarks, whereas the genuine are very little postmarked. The genuine stamps have a thread made in the paper down the middle of the stamp, and the only practicable way to detect these forgeries is by taking off the paper which is affixed to the back of the stamp (which may be done by soaking the stamp in warm water, when it will easily come off), and the thread will be found to be inserted between the stamp and the paper.

1864.—$1\frac{1}{4}$ *sch. blue.*

This stamp is well imitated; in fact, the very water-mark in the paper is copied. The letters in the inscription are not so well done as in the genuine. The first stroke of the M in the inscription at bottom (4 S. R. M.) is very thin in the forgery. The H in H. R. Z. G. L. at the left side is not so large as the other letters and is badly formed.

DUTCH INDIES.

I hear of the 5 c. being forged, but as I have not yet seen a specimen, I must describe it from the description which was sent me. In the forgery the face of the king is not shaded, and on the collar and ear to the right there is very little shading. The forgery is not well executed, the shading being the worst, but it is well known the genuine is beautifully executed.

FINLAND.

ENVELOPES.—5 *kop blue,* 10 *kop rose; transversely oval.*

GENUINE.	FORGED.
The lines on the shield touch the outline above and below.	The lines do not touch the outline either above or below.
Round the left and right side of the crown are 9 dots.	Round the left and right side of the crown are 8 dots.

Same as above.—20 *kop black.*

This imitation appears to be of a greenish slate colour. Inside the wide end of the left hand horn, within two circles, is a thin mark, and at the top of it is a dot; this is not so in the genuine. The eight stars also are very badly done in the forgery.

FRANCE.

UNPAID LETTER LABELS, 1863.—15 *centimes à percevoir, square.*

The inscription in the forgery is rather irregular, and the V in purcevoir is like a U. It appears to be a badly printed lithograph.

GRANADA CONFEDERATION.

1860.—*Arms in circle;* 10 *c. cinnamon,* 20 *c. blue.*

The upper and middle compartments of the shield in the 10 c. forgery are divided by only *one* line, whilst in the genuine, by either *two* or *three* lines. This one difference, I think, will suffice for to detect the above. The other stamp is rather better executed, but the following deficiencies will be found:—The white dots round the circle are not of a uniform size, and the two stars, one at each end of the bottom inscription, are very much *unlike* each other. The right side one looks like a cross with a dot at the left hand top corner and a smaller one at the opposite corner.

1861.—*Arms in shield;* $2\frac{1}{2}$ *cents black,* 5 *c. buff,* 10 *c. blue,* 20 *c. red,* 1 *peso rose.*

Genuine.	Forgery.
There are *nine* dots in the oval band containing shield.	There are only *eight* dots, one being in the centre, three on the left side, and four on the right.
There is a dot after *centavos.*	There is no dot after *centavos* excepting in the 5 c.
The 20 c. is printed in redy-brown.	It is printed in vermillion.

1862.—*Arms supported by wreath under nine stars; coloured impression,* 5 *cent orange,* 10 *c. blue,* 20 *c. red.*

In the forged 20 c. red the A of *Nacionales* is less than the other letters. The B also in *Columbia* is like a figure 8. The Na of *Nacionales* in the forged 5 c. is much less than the two end letters. In the forged 10 c. the letters E S in *Nacionales* touch each other, and the two right hand branches in the ornament at the right hand bottom corner touch each other. The above imitations have a forged look about them. The paper is very white and the ink very glaring.

GREAT BRITAIN.

Envelope, 1840.—*Vignette by W. Mulready, R.A.; upon the cover, coloured impression, rect.;* 1*d. black,* 2*d. blue.*

The engraving at the back of the envelope is entirely missed out of both the imitations. These are mostly sold by continental dealers, who would not, I think, hesitate to sell them to English collectors.

GREECE.

1862.—*Coloured impression on tinted paper,* 1 *lept light brown,* 2 *l. cinnamon,* 5 *l. green,* 10 *l. red,* 20 *l. blue,* 40 *l. violet,* 80 *l. rose.*

Genuine.	Forged.
The circle round the dots is of the same thickness, and very distinct throughout.	The circle is very thin, and in most places very indistinct.
The dots in the circle round the head of Mercury number 88.	The dots number about 75.
The letters and Greek border are of equal thickness.	The letters and Greek border are of variable thickness.

HAMBURG.

1859.—*Arms behind every figure indicating value; ½ sch. black, 1 sch., chocolate, 2 sch. red, 3 sch. blue, 4 sch. green, 7 sch. orange, 9 sch. yellow.*

1863.—*1¼ schilling mauve, 2½ green.*

GENUINE.	FORGED.
In all of them the thin upper stroke in the K in Postmarke is longer than the lower one.	The thin upper stroke is in all cases less than the thick lower one.
In the ½ the dot above I of Ein is the same size as the dot after schilling.	The dot after schilling is about twice as large as the other.
In the ½ also the A of Hamburg does not touch the M.	The base of the A touches the M.

HANOVER.

1858.—*Name Hannover, figure under crown, 3 pfennige rose; also same pattern 3 pf. green.*

GENUINE.	FORGED.
The lettering and crown is clear and well defined.	The inscription and crown is badly printed, being very much smudged.
The figure 3 is well shaped.	The figure 3 is badly shaped.
There is shading at the ends of the band holding inscription.	Instead of shading there is only smudged blotches.

INDIA.

1854.—*Head of Queen to left, ½ anna red.*

There are three imitations of this very rare stamp. The first is simply the comparatively common 1 anna of the same issue with the value erased, and "half" neatly painted in its place. The ornaments in the corners of these two stamps being different, this may easily be detected by comparing with the common 1 anna. The second imitation is printed from a forged block, and it may be detected in the same way as the above, as it appears to have been copied from the above-mentioned imitation. The other forgery is a very good one and I therefore append full description.

GENUINE.	FORGED.
The two A's of Anna are square at the top.	The two A's of Anna are pointed at the top.
The marks in the side borders are pretty large and triangular shaped.	The marks are small circular dots.
The inside white border is not narrow.	The inside white border is very narrow.

Same design, 1 anna red.

This forgery is too new looking, and the red is over bright.

IONIAN ISLANDS.

1860.—½*d. yellow*, 1*d. blue*, 2*d. lake, value not indicated.*

These forgeries are very blotched, and the inscription is irregularly printed. The last N in Ionikon is only about half the size of the first, and the two I's are not the same size. The collector has little chance of being mistaken in the identity of these forgeries.

LA GUAIRA.

1864.—*Name*, ½ *real pink*, 2 *reals green*

Genuine.	Forged.
The Q of Paquete has a long curved tail.	There is hardly any tail.
The O in Cabello is round.	The O is circular.
The waves are nicely engraved.	The waves do not seem to be well done.
The 8 in right hand top corner in the 2 r is well shaped.	The 8 is badly shaped, and appears like a piece of ornament.

LIBERIA.

Name, Figure of Liberty seated in circle; 6 *cents pink*, 12 *c. blue*, 24 *c. green.*

Genuine.	Forged.
The clouds are very distinct.	In the 6 c. and 24 c. the clouds are scarcely visible.
The C in cents is *not* under LI of Liberia in the 12 c.	The C *is* directly under the LI of Liberia.
In the 6 c. the toe of Britannia does *not* touch the border.	The toe *touches* the border.
Part of the postmark is the word *Monrovia.*	This part of the postmark is *Monrowa.*

The same set of stamps are forged at another place, but are not so well executed. The shading on the rock in the forgery touches the BE of Liberia, and it may be observed that in all three stamps the lines of the background run the same way, but not so in the genuine.

The 12 cent stamp numbers three imitations. In the third one the following differences may be detected :—In the genuine a full view of the face of Britannia is given, but in the forged it is turned to the left. The C in Cents is directly under B of Liberia in the forged, but it is not so in the genuine.

LIVONIA.

Briefmarke, red impression with inscription in black on white paper.

Pakenmarke, same design with green impression.

In the forged green stamp the first K in Packenmarke is rather badly shaped, the bottom of the short part being not quite on a level with the front and long mark. The lines in the background are also blotched. The small white cross at the left hand bottom corner is not quite finished in the forged red stamp, as the right hand bottom stroke is wanting. The other small crosses are also badly finished.

Red impression, green centre.

The colour of this imitation is bright, but the ink with which it is printed appears to be very poor; whereas in the genuine the ink is very good. The small white stars in each corner in the genuine have five distinct rays, but in the forgery the rays cannot be counted, being very indiscernible; indeed, the left hand bottom one appears to be a square white dot.

LUBECK.

1859.—*Name, ½ sch. violet, 1 sch. orange red, 2 sch. brown, 2½ sch. red, 4 sch. dark green.*

Genuine.	Forged.
There is a dot after *Postmarke.*	There is no dot after *Postmarke* in most of them.
There is no dot after *Schilling.*	In each stamp there is a dot after *schilling.*
The toe does not touch the line.	The right hand toe of the eagle touches the line just above the E of *Postmarke.*
In the ½ sch. there is shading after *Halber.*	The is no shading after *Halber.*
In the 1 sch. the eagle's tail is *not* pointed.	The eagle's tail *is* pointed.
The K of Lubeck in the 2 sch. does *not* touch the ornament on the side of it.	The K *does* touch the line.
The 2½ *has* shading by *zwei ein halber.*	There is *no* shading by *zwei ein halber.*
The shading of the riband in the 4 sch. is neat.	The shading of the riband is too thick.

There is another forged set of the above, but it may easily be detected on account of the letters of inscription being coarse and irregular in size.

LUXEMBURG.

1859-63.—*Name, arms in circle, 1 centime buff, 2 c. black, 4 c. yellow.*

The roughly executed forgeries of these stamps correspond with each other in the principal distinctions; therefore if any one has a genuine stamp of either three (all of which are very common when genuine), they will easily be detected by comparison. The forgeries have a line running up the side, and are printed on thin paper.

Name, arms in oval, 10 c. blue, 12½ c. rose, 25 c. marone, 30 c. violet, 37½ c. green, 40 c. vermillion.

Genuine.	Forged.
The letters UX of Luxembourg do not touch each other at any part..	The letters UX touch each other at top.
The paper is not thin.	The paper is very thin.
The thick stroke in the first U in *Luxembourg* is of equal thickness throughout.	The thick stroke in the U is rather thicker at the top than the bottom.

MAURITIUS.

1857.—*Value not indicated, red, dark green, magenta, slate.*

These stamps are evidently imitated by the same person that forged the Barbadoes stamps without date, and the same discrepances may be observed. The colours also are not correct having a washy look.

MEXICO.

1857.—2 *reals green on white paper.*

Genuine.	Forged.
The name of the issuing State is printed in black on the right side of the stamp.	No name is printed at all on the side of the stamp.
The background is composed of lines close together.	The background is solid.
The ornaments at sides are neatly done.	The ornaments at sides are badly done.

Same issue.—½ *real blue,* 1 *rl. yellow,* 2 *rs. green,* 4 *rs. red,* 8 *rs. violet.* 1861 *issue.—Black impression on coloured paper,* ½ *rl.,* 1 *rl.,* 2 *rs.,* 4 *rs. red on yellow,* 8 *rs. green on brown, and several more of the same design, but fictitious colours. In all* 20 *varieties.*

The colouring of the above imitations is extremely poor and thin, and the lettering very indistinct and irregular. The top inscription is *Medico* instead of *Megico.* They are, in fact, so poorly executed that it is utterly impossible for them to victimize collectors.

MODENA.

Inscription : *Poste Estense, eagle under crown,* 5 *c. green,* 9 *c. b. g. violet,* 10 *c. rose,* 10 *c. brown,* 15 *c. violet,* 15 *c. yellow,* 25 *c. primrose,* 40 *c. blue,* 1 *lira white.*

Genuine.	Forged.
The claws of the eagle are both alike, and have only three toes.	The claws are represented by four short thick strokes pointing downwards.
The letters of *cent* are short and thick.	The letters of cent are long and thin.
The ornaments at the right and left hand borders curl round at the ends.	The ornaments do not curl round at the ends.
Printed on unglazed paper.	Printed on glazed paper.

The above are poor imitations and I could name many more differences, but those mentioned will suffice. The above stamps are also forged a second time, and appear to be better executed, so that I append description.

Genuine.	Forged.
The crown *does not* touch the head of eagle.	The crown *touches* the head of eagle.
The tail of eagle *does not* touch the legs.	The tail *touches* the legs.
The eagle is properly shaped, and the feathers are neatly imitated.	The eagle is badly shaped, especially about the neck, which is too thick, and the feathers are blotchy.

PROVISIONAL GOVERNMENT.

1859.—*Arms (cross on shield), between two laurel branches, 5 cents green, 15 c. purple, 20 c. violet, 40 c. rose, 80 c. orange.*

Genuine.	Forged.
The corners are divided into equal sizes by the cross.	The lowest right hand corner is less than the others.
The point at the bottom of the shield is at the middle of the upright white line in the cross.	The point is more to the left at the bottom of the white line.
The cross on the ball at the top of crown is very indistinct, and some distance from the border line.	The cross on the ball is very clear and nearly touches the line.

Newspaper Label.—*Inscription "Tassa Gazette" encircling eagle; black impression,* 10 *cents.*

Genuine.	Forged.
Printed on unglazed paper.	Printed on glazed paper.
Printed from a wood block, and having a blotched and half finished appearance.	Lithographed, and the lines and inscription very neat.

MONTE VIDEO.

Second issue.—Name, arms in circle; 120 *cents blue,* 180 *c. green,* 240 *c. carmine.*

The forgeries under notice do not require a full description, as they are so badly executed and blotched in appearance, that it is impossible for them to deceive collectors. The ornaments in the corners are hardly perceptible, and the glory round the head is extremely blotched.

Same as above; 240 *cents carmine.*

This is better executed than the above, but the colouring is too thin and poor. The four dots at the right hand top corner are much lower down than the opposite ones. The inscription all around also touches the lines above and below.

1859.—60 *cents lilac, slate, brown, and pink.*

The following is the principal errors in this imitation, viz: the accent over the E in *Centisinias* is wanting—the ornaments in the corners are too large—and the letters of "Correo" on both sides of the stamp are thin and irregular in size.

Same issue.—80 *cents orange,* 180 *c. green,* 240 *c. red.*

Genuine.	Forged.
The letters EVID in Montevideo do not touch any where.	The letters EVID all touch one another at the top.
The ornament between the corner ornament and the M of Montevideo is as clear and well defined as the one between Correo and the same corner ornament.	The ornament is in most cases a thick stroke, but it is never so large and well shaped as the other one.

NEVIS.

1861.—*Name, 1 d. lake.*

GENUINE.	FORGED.
The letters of Nevis are a fair size.	The letters are unreasonably large.
The left arm of the female supporting the fainting one is held out straight to the standing one.	The left arm is turned up to the standing female.
There is a mineral spring coming from a rock in the back-ground.	There is no mineral spring, and the rock is represented by wavy lines all pointing downwards.

NEW BRUNSWICK.

1861.—*Name, coloured impression; 12½ c. blue (steam vessel.)*

The engraver of this forgery evidently worked from a description, and I cannot congratulate him on his success. The steamship has no paddles, but is apparently propelled by a screw. The colour is also much fainter than the genuine one.

ESSAY.—*Name, bust of Connell (formerly Postmaster-General), black impression on greyish paper.*

There are two imitations of this stamp, one of which is beautifully printed on India paper, and it may be detected by putting a drop of water on the stamp, when it will run as on blotting paper. The other imitation is a French photograph which may be detected in the same way as the 1 kr. black, Bavaria. (See Bavaria.)

NEW SOUTH WALES.

View of Sydney, coloured impression on white paper, 1d. red, and 2d. pale blue.

In the forgeries the first I of Siegillum is shorter than the S, and it appears to touch the line above it; the S touches the line beneath it. In the bottom right hand corner there is a square enclosing a cross, and in each corner of the square there is a small stroke, but the stroke in the right hand top corner in the same square is thicker than the others and blotched.

NICARAGUA.

1862.—*Name, coloured impression, 2 centavos blue, 5 c. black.*

GENUINE.	FORGED.
The letters are remarkably clear.	The letters are indistinct.
The U and A of Nicaragua just touch.	The U and A of Nicaragua are a reasonable distance from each other.
The figures in the corners are all alike.	The figures in the corners differ very much.
The letters of Centavos are all the same size, except the I, which is a trifle larger, and the bottom of V is flat.	The letters are not all same size, and the bottom of V is pointed.

The 5 c. is also forged at another place, and printed on India paper; it may be detected by putting a drop of water on the paper, when it will run like as on blotting paper.

NIE CALIDONIA.

1860.—*Name; 10 centimes grey.*

GENUINE.	FORGED.
The front part of the neck does not touch the border.	The front part of the neck touches the border.
Many of the letters of both top and bottom inscriptions touch at both top and bottom the lines enclosing them.	The letters of Nie Calodonie only touch the top line enclosing them, and 10 c. Postes, only touches the bottom line.
The forehead touches the border enclosing the head.	The forehead does not touch the border.

The photographs of this stamp, which are sold by French dealers, may be detected in the same manner as the black Bavaria.

NORWAY.

1850.—*Inscription: Frimærke, arms in a circle, coloured impression, 4 skilling blue.*

In this forgery the lettering is small and indistinct, the colour light blue ultramarine, and is printed by lithography, generally postmarked, and the postmark is far too clearly defined and printed.

OLDENBURG.

1852.—*Name, black impression on coloured paper, $\frac{1}{30}$ thaler blue, $\frac{1}{15}$ thaler rose, and $\frac{1}{10}$ thaler yellow.*

GENUINE.	FORGED.
The bottom edge of the mantle (surrounding the shield), is formed by very small dots.	The bottom edge is formed by rather large dots on the right side.
In the $\frac{1}{15}$ the point of the small upper shield is over the right side of the figure 1 of $\frac{1}{15}$.	The point of the small shield is just over the centre of the figure 1.
The shading in the band, in the $\frac{1}{30}$ is very perceptible.	The shading is very indistinct in the band in the right hand lower portion.
The figure 1 in the $\frac{1}{15}$ stamp above 15 is in the middle of the divisional line.	There is a larger portion of the divisional line of $\frac{1}{15}$ to the *right* of the figure 1 than the left.

All the above, also 1858 issue, $\frac{1}{3}$ gros green, 1 gros blue, 2 gr. rose, 3 gr. yellow. 1860 issue, $\frac{1}{4}$ gr. orange, $\frac{1}{3}$ green, $\frac{1}{2}$ redbrown.

These forgeries are wretchedly executed. The genuine are neatly designed and executed, but these are miserable lithographs. The inscription is bad and irregular, the colouring bad, the printing smudgy, and hardly any shading in the whole lot.

OTTOMAN EMPIRE.

Name in Turkish characters inscribed in a crescent; black impression on coloured paper; 20 *paras yellow,* 1 *piastre lilac,* 2 *piastres blue,* 5 *piastres rose.*

These forgeries may be detected by a close examination of the Turkish character in the crescent immediately beneath the Sultan's autograph. The imitation of the Turkish inscription consists merely of dots and flourishes, but without the slightest semblance of the original.

PARAGUAY.

These stamps are very mysterious, as it is not really known whether they were ever issued, or whether they are simply essays. Out of the four best catalogues that are published, two call them essays and the other two mention 3 stamps as being issued for postal uses. As it is not required of me to give any opinion respecting that moot point, my purpose merely being to detect forgeries, I must give a description of six of them which I know to be forgeries. The colours are respectively red, green, grey, black, yellow, and brown. The stars in the corners are badly formed; the lettering on inscription also is badly executed, the letters being thin and smudged. The pole above the lion's head is represented by a white mark; and the circle of dots at the right side of the oval are larger than those on the left.

PARMA.

First issue.—Coloured impression on white paper, 5 *ce. yellow,* 15 *c red; black impression on coloured paper,* 5 *c. yellow,* 15 *c. red.*

GENUINE.	FORGED.
The stamps are very smudgy, especially the coloured impression ones.	They are very clearly printed.
The background consists of white crossed lines, which makes it appear like small square dots.	The background is composed of rather rough looking large and small dots.

PROVISIONAL GOVERNMENT.

1859.—*Coloured impression on white paper,* 5 *c. green,* 10 *c. brown,* 20 *c. blue,* 40 *c. red,* 80 *c. orange; black impression,* 6 *c. carmine,* 9 *c. blue.*

GENUINE.	FORGED.
All the lines forming the border are concave.	The 4 short lines, are quite straight, and the four longer ones concave.
The middle line in the border is nearer to the outside than to the inside line.	The middle line is nearer to the inside line.
The lines are rather broken.	The lines are too sharp and neat.

PONY EXPRESS.

1, 2, 3, *and* 4 *dollars all in five colours.*

There are two separate forgeries of these stamps, but the first with which I will treat are the Hamburg emanations and which are the most widely circulated. In the forgery the second thin stroke in the N in Pony is thinner than the first. In the genuine the breath is shown to issue out of the horses nostrils, but nothing of the sort is perceptible in the imitation. These two differences I think will suffice for the above. In the other imitations the breath which ought to issue out of horses nostrils cannot be seen, and the P in *Pony* is badly shaped. The ornamentation in the corners also is very blotchy and badly defined.

PRUSSIA.

ENVELOPES, 1851.—*Head of King; 7 s. gr. vermillion.*

GENUINE.	FORGED.
Colour is vermillion.	Colour, dull red.
The two threads across the stamp are worked in the paper.	The threads are inserted between the embossed paper and some thin paper pasted on the back.
On the neck of the King there is the word *Schilling* in very small letters.	The word *Schilling* is wanting.

ROMAGNA.

1860.—½ *bai yellow*, 1 *grey*, 2 *yellow*, 3 *dark green*, 4 *red*, 5 *lilac*, 6 *green*, 8 *rose*, 20 *blue.*

GENUINE.	FORGED.
The paper is rather coarse, and the colour is not shiny.	The paper is very glaring in colour and pretty fine and smooth.
The two dots after Bai: are square.	The two dots after BAI: are round.

ROMAN STATES.

Inscription: Franco Bollo Postale; 50 *baj. blue.*

In this stamp there is a rather large ornament in each corner, and in the ornament there is two short lines running from the corner and pointing towards the centre of the stamp. In the forgery this is correct in three corners, but in the left hand bottom corner there is only one stroke in the ornament, and the other stroke is represented by a very small dot touching the enclosing line. In the genuine the letters TAL of *Postale* touch each other at the bottom, but in the forgery the letters TA only touch each other.

SANDWICH ISLANDS.

1860.—*Inscription : Inter Island Hawaiian Postage ;* 1 *c. blue, black,* 2 *c. blue, black.*

The simple design of these stamps render imitation very easy, and the forgeries I am about to describe being very close copies, it is extremely difficult to detect them. The large figure 2 in the 2 c. is thicker in the original than in the forgery, whilst the C in the 1 cent is very broad, but only moderately broad in the imitation. In the 2 c. forgery the tail of the 2 projects a little outwards, with a rounded turn, but in the genuine the tail does not point out any further than on a level with the back of the 2, and it is perfectly, straight, not being curved as in the forgery. In the genuine 1 cent the letters are all pretty thin and neat, especially the 1, which has a long and thick stroke at the top. In the forgery the letters are thicker and rather smudged, and the stroke on the top of 1 is very thin and much shorter than the genuine.

Name Honolulu, bust of King, 5 *c. blue.*

Genuine.	Forged.
The whole face is thickly dotted, excepting the nose.	There is a small white place under the left side of mouth which is not dotted.
The six buttons on the king's coat on the left side of the leaves are very distinct and white.	These buttons are very indistinct and four can be perceived.

Same as above.—13 *c. red.*

This forgery is lithographed, but the genuine is printed from steel dies. In the genuine the figure 8 in the right hand space is on a level with the letters of States, but in the forgery it is above. There is no dot after the words "United States" in the forgery, but there is a dot in the genuine.

SAXONY.

1850.—*Name Sachsen ;* 3 *pfennige red.*

There are two imitations of this stamp; the first, which I now describe, is decidedly the worst executed, and may be detected by a close observation of the ornamentation in the large figure 3. In the genuine it is composed of ornaments very like small figures 3. The other and better imitation I more fully describe.

Genuine.	Forged.
The word Pfennige is printed in the centre of the side label.	The word Pfennige is too high, as there is more space below than above it.
There is a stop after Franco.	No stop after Franco.
The ornamentation in the background touches the figure.	There is a white margin all round the figure.

1851.—*Head of King to right in oval; printed in black on coloured paper, 1 n. gr. rose, 2 n. gr. blue, 3 n. gr. yellow.*

These are very like Messrs. Spiro Brother's lithographs, but they appear to come from Liverpool, only in very small quantities however, and almost totally obliterated with post marks.

Genuine.	Forged.
At both ends of the label enclosing Sachsen there is, more or less, some very fine shading.	It is not shaded here, but there is a solid mass which was perhaps intended for the shading.
The ground within the oval when closely examined will be found to form fine lines very close together, so much so, that it appears to be solid.	This background in the oval is entirely solid.
The numerals of value at sides and bottom are all one size in each respective stamp.	The figure of value at bottom in the 1 n. gr. is less than the others, but in the other two stamps it is larger than the side ones.

SPAIN.

First issue.—Bear on tree, and printed in bronze, 1 *cuartos,* 2 *c., and* 3 *c.*

Genuine.	Forged.
The centre band contains seven dots or stars.	The band only contains five dots.
The band enclosing bear and tree is oval shaped.	The band is quite circular.

The above is a very poor imitation and I might name many more distinctions. There is another and better set of forgeries in the market, which I now also describe.

Genuine.	Forged.
There are two small ornaments below the third bunch of leaves on the left hand side.	There is only one ornament below the bunch.
There is a star in the oval, exactly opposite the above small ornament.	This star is on a level with the top of the leaves of the bunch, below the third bunch.

1850.—6 *cuartos black.*

This is an exceedingly bad imitation, being badly lithographed and printed. The original is pretty well engraved, and the inscription is regular in size and thickness. The ink with which the imitation is printed is very thin and not so black as the genuine.

1851.—2 *reals red.*

This fac-simile, although executed by the same persons as the above, is about the best Spanish forgery extant. The colour is not what would be desirable, yet the printing is very good and neat. In the genuine the ornaments in all the four corners are like each other, but in the imitation there is considerable difference both in size and shape.

1851.—6 *c. black.*

This is one of Spiro's worst imitations, suffice it is to say that in the forgery the C of Cuartos is only half the size of the R, and that all the corner ornaments are blotched. The next is the

1852.—5 *reales green.*

Genuine.	Forged.
The ornaments are all alike in the angles.	The ornament in the right side lower angle is incomplete.
There is a stop after Correos.	There is no stop after Correos.
The first O of Correos is smaller than the second.	The first O is larger than the second.

1853.—5 *reales green.*

Genuine.	Forged.
The small circles round the oval are all of equal sizes	These circles vary in size.
The C of Correos is on a level with the other letters of that word.	The C appears to the naked eye to be almost touching the line underneath, and it is lower down than the other letters.

1855.—6 *c. red.*

There are two different forgeries of this stamp. In one the letters of inscription are thin, in the other thick. In the best looking imitation the A and N of Franco touch each other at the base, and the lines in the corners outside the oval are very thick and far between. In the other imitation, which is an emanation from Hamburg; the colouring is very washy looking, and the Queen's head is very unnatural looking. There is only a few dots on the left side of the neck and none about the chin.

1854.—5 *reales green.*

In this imitation the bottom half of the figure 8 is larger than the upper one, but in the genuine they are equal in size; another noticeable feature is the 4 in 1854, which is longer than the other three figures.

Official Labels, 1854.—$\frac{1}{2}$ *onza orange,* 1 *rose,* 4 *green,* 1 *libra blue.*

Genuine.	Forged.
In the $\frac{1}{2}$ and 4 there is a large dot after the word onza.	This dot is extremely small.
In the left lower quarter of the shield the lion's right front leg is composed of two thin lines.	The lion's leg is formed of only one rather thick stroke.
The cross on the top of the crown does not touch the line above; in the 1 onza it appears to the naked eye to do so, but it really does not.	The cross touches the line in all the four stamps.

1855.—*Oval;* $\frac{1}{2}$ *orange,* 1 *rose,* 4 *green,* 1 *libra blue.*

Genuine.	Forged.
The C of Official evidently touches the I after it.	The C does not touch the I anywhere.
The stamp is very clearly shaded.	It is not remarkably clear, in some places rather coarse.

SPANISH POSSESSIONS

CUBA, HAYTI, AND PORTO RICO.

1857.—*Laureated Head of Queen Isabella II. to right in circle, printed in colour on white paper, ½ rl. plata f. blue, 1 rl. plata f. green, 2 rl. plata rose.*

GENUINE.	FORGED.
The number of small white dots round the edge of the circle enclosing Queen's head, is 73.	The number of white dots is 68.
The small ornaments in each corner are round	The ornaments are no uniform shape at all, some being square, some triangular, some like stars, and others a mere blotch.
In the top frame at each end of the inscription, is a white dot.	This dot is at neither end of the inscription in the ½, and it is only at one end in the 2 rl. plata.

SWITZERLAND.

FEDERAL ADMINISTRATION.

1850.—*Black impression,* 5 *rappen,* 10 *rap.*

1852.—*Same device,* 5 *rap·,* 15 *rap.*

GENUINE.	FORGED.
The letters of Rayon do not touch each other anywhere.	The letters of Rayon nearly all touch one another at the base.
The four ends of the cross are all about one size.	The right side end of the cross is decidedly the least.

In addition to these two points, the forgeries are all so covered with obliterating marks that the design of the stamps can hardly be seen, whilst in the genuine, although they are sometimes well postmarked, yet the design is almost always wholly perceptible.

GERMAN AND FRENCH CANTONS.

Inscription : Poste Locale, 2½ *rappen.*

In this stamp there is a small perpendicular line under 2½ aud R P, but in the imitation it is omitted. The paper on which the forgery is printed appears to be of a blueish colour, whereas in the genuine it is white.

BASLE.

Inscription : Stadt Post Basel,, 2½ *rap green.*

This forgery is neatly executed, and the surest test for detecting it, is by observing the ground. In the genuine it is formed of alternate blue and white dots, whereas in the forgery it is composed of a ground, uniform blue.

GENEVA.

There are forgeries of all the Geneva stamps issued, and owing to the considerable differences between the genuine ones, it makes it impossible to give a description of any differences which may exist between the original and the imitations. The only sure way of detecting one or two of them is by observing the paper, the genuine 5 cent green is printed on white paper, but the forgery is printed on rather bluish tinted paper. The genuine 5 c. dark green is on extremely dark blue paper. The other forgeries are impossible to detect without they are submitted to some one who is well conversant with forgeries. The following is a description of Spiro's emanations:—The UX of Lux touch each other at the top. The shading round INS at the top is blotchy. The second E in Tenebras is larger than the first. The end of the band containing inscription above the shield touches the enclosing line at the right hand side, but not at the left.

NEUFCHATEL.

Inscription: Poste Locale, white cross on red ground, 5 *cents.*

GENUINE.	FORGED.
The label containing inscription above the cross is some distance from the top, and the two three pointed ornaments at each end of the label are *not* so broad as the label.	The label is very close to the top, and the three pointed ornaments are as broad as the label.

VAUD.

Same as above with Post Horn, 4 *c., and* 5 *c., black impression.*

GENUINE.	FORGED.
The top of the post horn on the right side is slightly turned outwards, and the left end of it almost touches the border of the scroll.	The top of the horn is turned inwards, and the left end of it is further off the scroll.
The letters of inscription Poste Locale are long and neat.	The letters are short and rather blotchy.

WINTERTHUR.

Inscription: Orts-Post, Poste-Locale, 2½ *rappen, black impression.*

This is a very nicely executed *fac-simile.* There are two varieties of the genuine, one with the horn longer than the other. In the forgery there is no stop after the word Post, and the rope or chain holding up the cross is composed of six circles. The genuine has a stop after Post, and the chain holding up the cross is composed of eight circles or links.

ZURICH.

1843. Essays.—4 *and* 6 *rappen, name, large figure indicating value.*

In the above forgeries the horizontal red strokes that are painted over the large figure and the background, are more numerous and nearer together on the left side of the large figure than on the right; in fact there are about two to one. All the imitations I have seen are post marked, but I am assured that no stamps were issued in Switzerland until 1850, so the above can only be essays.

1856.—*Name;* 4 *rappen, Local Taxe.*

There are two imitations of this stamp. The first (Spiro's) has the T of "Taxe" almost touching the line above, and the whole letters of "Local Taxe" are smudged. In the top right corner there is a small square with five dots; the middle dot is about twice the size of the others. The X in "Taxe" is not so large as the E following.

In the other forgery, which is better executed, there is no hyphen between the words "Local Taxe," but in the genuine there is. The small semi-circles and ornaments in the border, and also the four corner squares, are much thicker and darker than the rest of the stamp, whereas in the genuine all the circles are of the same thickness, both in the border and in the corner squares.

Cantonal Taxe, 6 *rappen.*

Spiro's imitation of this stamp may be detected by observing that the hyphen joining the words "Cantonal Taxe" is omitted, and the three top ornaments and semi-circles in the border at the right side are much larger than the three top ones on the opposite side.

The other imitation shows the following inaccuracies, viz: there is no hyphen joining the words "Local Taxe," it is printed on rather blue glazed paper," the border is composed of four thin lines. In the genuine there is a hyphen joining "Local Taxe," and it is printed on rather dirty white unglazed paper. The border is composed of three thin black lines.

TRINIDAD.

Value not indicated, crimson, blue slate.

These forgeries are exceedingly bad lithographs. The characters and inscription are too small, and the colours very thin and poor.

TUSCANY.

Lion on white paper, 1 *quattr*, 1 *soldo*, 1 *crazier*, 2 *cra.*, 4 *cra.*, 6 *cra.*, 9 *cra.*, (*Provisional Government*), 5 *cent*, 10 *c.*, 20 *c.*, 40 *c.*, 80 *c.*

Genuine.	Forged.
On rather coarse and unglazed paper.	On very smooth paper.
There is a water mark in the paper.	There is no water mark in the paper.
In the Provisional Government stamps there is a cross on the top of the crown.	The cross is hardly perceptible.

There is another forgery of the 1 quattr black, which would have been pretty well executed had the left hand inscription (Franco Bollo) not been left out. It is usually sold as a rarity.

TWO SICILIES.

SICILY.

1859.—½ *gr. orange*, 1 *gr. olive*, 2 *gr. blue*, 5 *gr. red*, 10 *gr. dark blue*, 20 *gr. black*, 50 *gr. dark red.*

There are two forged sets of the above stamps In the first set I describe, it appears that the forger has only had a part of the set to forge the whole seven stamps from.

No. 1 FORGERIES.

Genuine.	Forged.
In the half gr. the numeral of value is like this ½.	The half is like this ½.
The colour of the 1 gr. is orange, and the 50 gr. is dark red.	Both these stamps are coloured red.
There is a dot after Sicilia in the whole set.	There is no dot after Sicilia.
The background is formed of rather rough crossed lines.	The background in some of them is solid.

No. 2 FORGERIES.

Genuine.	Forged.
The B of Bollo does not reach as far as the corner of the border enclosing the head.	Part of the B comes past the left hand corner of the border enclosing the head.
The background is composed of crossed lines.	The background is quite solid.
The dot after Sicilia is generally wanting, always very indistinct.	This dot is always very distinct.

PROVISIONAL GOVERNMENT.

October 1860.—½ *tornese blue.*

In this forgery there is wanting a small G, which ought to be in the bottom white line almost under the half. The head which ought to be at the juncture of the three legs is also wanting.

November, 1860 —½ *tornese blue.*

The small G which is wanting in the above forgery is also omitted in this, and in the genuine the outline of the three legs and fleur-de-lis as in the first issue, can be seen, but it is rather indistinct, whereas in the forgery no traces of anything of the sort can be observed. There are two imitations of this stamp. The other is by the Hamburg forgers, and is a very poor imitation; it may be detected in the same manner as the above. I may also say that the inscription is very irregular and blotched.

NAPLES.

1857.—½ *grano*, 1 *gr.*, 2 *gr.*, 5 *gr.*, 10 *gr.* 20 *gr.*, 50 *gr.*; *printed in lake on white paper.*

Genuine.	Forged.
Printed on rough coarse looking paper.	Printed on fine white smooth paper.
The horse's mane is composed of a white clear space like the neck, with a line to divide the mane from the neck.	The horse's mane is thickly shaded.
The three fleurs-de-lis are all much like each other.	There is more or less difference in all the stamps between the three fleurs-de-lis, some are smaller than others, or some are not so clear as others.

VENEZUELA.

1863.—*Eagle in circle*, ½ *real yellow*, 1 *rl. blue*, 2 *rls. green.*

Genuine.	Forged.
There is a dot after Real.	There is no dot after Real.
The letters of Real are not so large as those of Federation.	The letters of Real are of the same size and thickness as those of Federation.
None of the letters of Venezaluna touch the line of the scroll underneath.	Some of the letters touch the line.

WESTERN AUSTRALIA.

Name, a swan naiant, 1*d. black*, 2*d. pink*, 2*d. blue*, 6*d. green*, 6*d. brown red.*

Genuine.	Forged.
All the letters are flat at the ends.	Nearly all the letters are round and pointed at the ends and badly engraved.
The background is very elaborately executed.	Background consists of straggling dots.
The letters of inscription are very regular in size and shape.	The letters are somewhat irregular in shape, especially the A's in Postage and Australia, no two being alike.

WURTEMBURG.

1850.—*Square inscription: Wurtemburg,* 1 *kreuzer buff,* 3 *kr. yellow,* 6 *kr. green,* 9 *kr. rose.*

GENUINE.	FORGED.
At the top of the U in Wurtemburg, there *are two* dots.	In the 3 kr. there is only *one*, and in the other stamps there is *none*.
The ornaments just outside of the diamond touch, or nearly always touch, the corners of the inner square.	The ornaments are a good distance from the corner.
There is a dot after the large figure 3 in the diamond.	There is no dot after the figure 3,

1850.—*Name;* 18 *kr. neutral.*

This is a very good imitation as regards execution, but the colour of the paper is reddish purple instead of neutral. The number of lines from the top to the bottom are 23, but there are 25 in the genuine.

RETURNED LETTER LABEL.—*Inscription: Commission Für Retourbriefe; black.*

The forged emanation from Hamburg of this stamp is beautifully lithographed. In the genuine there is a dot after "Retourbriefe," but it is omitted in this fac-simile. The two lower ornaments in the forgery between the oval and the square ornament in the corner are very unlike each other in shape.

There is another imitation of this stamp which is bad to detect; in it, however, the dot after "Retourbriefe" is omitted, and it is printed on white paper, whereas it must be remembered that the genuine is in all cases on white paper with a bluish tinge in it.

ADDENDA.

The following counterfeits have come under notice too late for insertion in their proper places.

BADEN.

1855.—*Inscription: Baden Freimarke,* 1 *kreuzer white.*

GENUINE.

The minute inscriptions at sides are very neatly executed.

The corner ornaments are all *like* each other in size and shape and neatly executed.

The lettering of Friemarke is a uniform size, and neat and regular.

FORGED.

The inscriptions at sides are exceedingly poorly done, and it is utterly impossible to read them.

The corner ornaments are very much *unlike* each other, and badly done.

The first R in Freimarke is larger than the second R, and the whole word is carelessly executed.

BRAZIL,

1861.—*Oblong Roman figures indicating value, printed in black,* 10 *reis,* 20, 30, 90, 180.

GENUINE.

The figures are very distinct, especially the black shading.

The outside enclosing line is very straight and well defined in the whole set.

The numeral of value is in all the stamps well shaped.

FORGED.

The black shading of the figures is not well defined and it runs into the background.

This line is crooked and broken in several places; in the right hand top corner of most of the stamps it runs into the line within it.

The 9 in the 90 reis is leaning towards the left and is very badly formed.

Probably the 300 and 600 reis of the same issue are forged, but I have not yet seen a specimen. I would however beg to caution collectors against the same, and if they are forged, which is very probable, the above description will no doubt suffice to detect them.

CORRIENTES.

I hear of the Corrientes stamp being forged, but I have not yet had an opportunity of seeing a copy. I understand, however, that the imitations are much better executed than the genuine, and that there is great dissimilarity in the paper. I merely mention this to put collectors on their guard against this *fac-simile*, but if they should see two copies of this stamp unlike each other, they need not conclude that one of them is forged or *vice versa*, as the genuine stamps are printed in plates of eight, and all of them are slightly different in design.

GERMANY.

NORTHERN STATES.

1850.—*Inscription*: *Freimarke, large numeral of value in square, printed in black on red brown paper,* $\frac{1}{4}$ *silb. grosch.*

Genuine.	Forged.
In each of the four corners of the inner square, there is a small shield with numeral of value thereon neatly executed.	The numeral of value on the shield is wretchedly done, in the two lower corners especially. In the left lower corner the mark between 1 and 4 thus ¼ is entirely missing, and in the opposite corner it bears no resemblance to a figure.
The small horns in the four corners are all very much alike.	These horns hardly resemble each other. The small end of the one in the top right corner is very short and blotchy, whilst the small end of the lower one on the same side is much larger.

There are several more differences, but the above will suffice. The forgery, although it appears at first sight to be an exceedingly good imitation, yet the execution bears no comparison with the genuine, the small letters on the sides not being near so well executed.

FICTITIOUS STAMPS

THE stamps I mention under this head, are:—

1. STAMPS WHICH NEVER EXISTED AS *BONA-FIDE* POSTAGE STAMPS, BUT WERE ORIGINATED BY FORGERS.

The first mentioned stamps are all purely imaginary, and appear to have been executed more for the inexperienced collector, than for the victimizing of Collectors in general. I think it is not requsite to give a full description of them, so I merely append a list, with sufficient descriptions however to detect them.

BAVARIA.—Figure 3 in a circle; black impression.

CAPRERA.—Inscription: Postal Capera Italin; 1 scudo.

CONFEDERATE STATES.—Head of Davis to right in oval; 5 c. red and black.

JAPAN.—Several stamps all different sizes and colours. Design, imitation of a French horn.

JERUSALEM.—Inscription in hieroglyphical figures, design Pyramids in square.

MEXICO.—Pretended stamp to frank from Acapulco in Mexico to San Francisco in California. Name, McRobish & Co.; blue and pink.

NASHVILLE.—5 c. grey.

TURKISH.—Crescent and star; 6 bronze olive 3 mura red. Golden fleece, letters, J. E. below.

U.S. MORMON STAMP.—Head of Brigham Young. Inscription: Utah five cents Postage; red and green.

U.S. LOCAL STAMPS.—Blood's Despatch, eagle and dove, Clinton's Penny Post Clark & Co.'s Box, Clemin's Dispatch, Cressman & Co.'s Penny Post, Carrier's 1 c. Despatch, De Ming's Penny Post, Davis & Co.'s Post, Floyd's Penny Post, G. Carter's Dispatch, Ker's City Post, Paid Eagle Post at Adam's Express, Priest's Dispatch, Royal Post, Steven's 1 c. Despatch, Well's Penny Post.

2. STAMPS WHICH WERE NEVER INTENDED FOR POSTAL USE.

The stamps in this class are those which were never intended for postal uses, but which are, however, designedly sold by dealers as *bona-fide* postage stamps. Some of them are Receipt and Bill stamps and some are trade labels, &c.

AUSTRIA.—Complimentary Labels, which are intended to fill up the proper number of stamps on a sheet—47 varieties.

BAVARIA.—The whole issues of 1851 and 1862 are printed in black, and are called "Tribers d'Instruction."

BERNE.—Name: Canton Berne, Bear on Shield; 10 rap yellow, 3 r. blue, Receipt stamps.

BRUNSWICK.—Stamps on the Receipts given for registered letters, 6 pf. red, lake, ½ gr. red.

DENMARK.—Inscription:—Thiele at sides; black impression.

FRANCE.—Several trade labels with Head of Emperor and French inscriptions.

GENEVA.—Man with spear leaning on a shield, various colours, Receipt stamps.

ICELAND.—Trade labels, various colours. Design: Bear in shield, Name: Vulneré.

JAMAICA.—Several Bill stamps.

OCEAN POSTAGE.—Six varieties. Inscription: Ocean Penny Postage, advertisements for bringing the universal system of the Ocean Penny Postage into notice.

ZURICH.—Various values, all Receipt stamps.

3. STAMPS WHICH HAVE BEEN CHANGED IN COLOUR BY CHEMICALS.

The stamps under this head are mostly comparatively common stamps, which have been changed in colour by a peculiar chemical process, and then sold as either rare undiscribed varieties, proofs, or essays. The only safe method to guard against such forgeries is, by refusing to buy any as such that are not mentioned in the best catalogues. I herewith append a list of all such stamps I have either met with or heard of.

ARGENTINE CONFED:—1861, 10 c. green changed to blue.
1850, 9 kr. blue changed to green.

AUSTRIA.—1858, Newspaper stamp, lavender changed to a dirty grey.

BADEN.—1850, 6 krs. green changed to yellow.
" 1855, 9 krs. pink changed to white.

BAVARIA.—1851, 9 krs. green changed to pale lemon.

BELGIUM.—1849, 20 c. blue changed to black.
" 1 c. to blue.

BREMEN.—1855, 5 grote pink to white.
" " 7 gr. yellow to grey.

BRITISH GUIANA, 1853, 4 c. blue to black.

BRUNSWICK.—1852, 2 s. gr. blue to black.

CONFEDERATE STATES.—1862, 10 c. blue to black.

FRANCE.—1854, 5 cents green to blue.
" " 20 c. blue to black.

GERMANY, SOUTH.—1860, 3 kr. blue to green.
" " 1 kreuzer to blue.
GREECE.—20 lepta blue to black.
HANOVER.—1858, 1 guten gr. green to yellow.
HOLLAND.—1852, 5 cents blue to black.
ITALY.—15 c. to green impression on yellow paper.
MODENA.—10 c. rose to violet (there is a 10 c. violet stamp, but most of those sold at present are chemical varieties.
NEWFOUNDLAND.—2nd issue, 3d. green to black.
NEW ZEALAND.—1d. dark brown.
NOVA SCOTIA.—1860, 1 cent black to green.
OLDENBURG.—1851, 1 silb. gr. green to yellow.
" 1858, $\frac{1}{3}$ gros. green to grey.
" " 2 " red to white.
" 1857, 2 s. gr. blue to black.
PRUSSIA.—1858, 4 pfug. green to blue.
" " 1 silb. gr. pink to white.
" " 3 silb. gr. yellow to grey.
ROMAGNA.—1851, 20 bai blue to black.
SAXONY.—1851, 1 n. gr. rose to white.
" " 2 n. gr. blue to black.
" " 3 n. gr. yellow to white.
SWITZERLAND.—Rayon II., 10 rappen yellow to slate colour.
UNITED STATES.—1861, 10 cent green to blue.
" " 1 cent blue to black.
WURTEMBERG.—1850, 9 krs. rose to white.
" 1860, 6 kr. green to blue.